Thank yo
me on you
show. I had a
inspired by the way
service in the forefront 'of
I would love to work u
some day!

Best,

Melanie
Feldman

BOLD

GET NOTICED GET HIRED

MELANIE FELDMAN
JOSHUA SIVA
LIZ MADSEN

TABLE OF CONTENTS

GETTING STARTED

We are three friends, entrepreneurs, and recent college graduates. Unfortunately, the small business ventures we started in college didn't turn into the next million-dollar idea, so we had to bite the bullet and find jobs after college. We all have different stories, but let us tell you, the process wasn't easy for any of us.

Not one company we applied for responded to us. We didn't understand; our resumes were impressive and we were all hard workers. We realized that common courtesy was a bygone, and hundreds of job applications later we all knew we had to change the way we applied for jobs. We weren't even being given a shot. No one was looking at our resumes, mainly because the stack was too big and ours were stuck somewhere in the middle.

We each had our own epiphanies that we were in a vicious cycle and had to get out. So with that, our focuses shifted. We no longer played the numbers game by applying for a hundred jobs each day with the hope that one returned a response. Instead, we focused on a few companies where we were actually interested in working. From there we used creative techniques to get our resume in front of a human being. These techniques varied from leveraging social media, tapping our alumni network, going bold in a cold email to ESPN sportscasters, and vigorously connecting with the right people on LinkedIn. After months spent applying for jobs and hearing nothing back, all of a sudden we had multiple interview requests flowing in each week. Instead of reading the morning news in our inbox, we had corporate communications groups trying to get in touch with us. The tables were now officially turned, and job-hunting was almost fun. (We said *almost*.)

The craziest part was this. These interviews came from the same companies and open positions to which we had previously applied; and we were using identical resumes. At the very least, our creativity was giving us a shot. So with our newfound courage and an overflowing inbox, it didn't take long for our friends to start asking what we were doing, and more importantly, how we had such badass jobs. To put this in context, we were applying back in 2010, as companies slashed and burned their own payrolls in an effort to stay afloat during the financial crisis. Curiosity amongst our network turned to persistent questioning. Our friends had to know how we landed our jobs, and of course we were happy to share our stories. They were shocked—most people reacted with, "Wow, I would have never thought to do that." And that, my friends, is exactly the problem.

Full of fuel to answer the "what" and "how" for everyone, we embarked on a journey to write a book to help those who are going through the same frustrations that we endured. Through real life examples, transparent detail, and a conversational dialogue, our number one goal is to educate you on different creative ways to apply for jobs. To make this happen, we set out to find unique and innovative techniques that others have used to land jobs. We spoke to people from all over the country and even around the world. We found stories online, through our own network, and by word of mouth, *and the results were amazing.* Nearly every person that we reached out to was willing to share his or her story. It certainly didn't hurt that we were applying some of the very techniques we write about here to get in touch, but that's just a minor detail!

Every interview we had, we walked away feeling inspired, and writing this book has been nothing short of an incredible story in itself. We hope that you find inspiration as well, and that you realize the frustrations you are feeling from the job hunt is not because of a lack of supply, but the way you're demanding. Trust us, it will all work out. You just have to give yourself a chance, be bold in doing so, so that you too can get noticed, and get hired.

Now of course, this book is about helping you, and not so much about learning our life histories or our favorite color (fun fact as a group: It's blue!), but here is a little background on the three of us:

Bold

Joshua Siva

Hometown: Buffalo, NY
College & Graduation: University of Pittsburgh, 2011
Current Job: IT Procurement Associate at GlaxoSmithKline
Current City: Philly
Coolest Thing I Did in College: Played in a rock band
How I Landed My Job: Alumni Network
Fun Fact: I've had several of my symphonies played by live orchestras

Melanie Feldman

Hometown: Honolulu, Hawaii
College & Graduation: University of Pittsburgh, 2011
Current Job: Publisher Development Coordinator at Undertone
Current City: New York, NY
Coolest Thing I Did in College: Played Division 1 volleyball
How I Landed My Job: Connected with people on LinkedIn
Fun Fact: I started an online website called bookzingo.com

Liz Madsen

Hometown: Pittsburgh (aka City of Champions)
College & Graduation: Carnegie Mellon, 2011
Current Job: Brand Strategist at Curalate
Current City: Philly
Coolest Thing I Did in College: Raised $10k in 3 weeks for a class project
How I Landed my Job: Twitter
Fun Fact: I bought a stick shift having never driven one before

Before we dive into the process of getting noticed and the different techniques you can deploy for this purpose, it's important to understand the value of your base.

We define the "Base" as the core content and materials that help define you. They represent your experiences, your personality, your character, and special powers (maybe not so much for the special powers, but if you have one let us know). In the professional world, they materialize as the following:

1. Resume
2. LinkedIn profile
3. Clean first page on Google
4. Social Presence (Twitter, Google+, etc.)

These items are essential because at the end of the day, no matter how creative you get or how much you "wow" someone, odds are that each one of these items will be referenced before a job offer can be made. Throughout this book, we'll be providing you tips on how to perfect these base items.

Lastly, there are a number of different options available when addressing the essential items and creative approaches you can take during your search. To help you along your journey, the book is broken into four main sections that guide you through these options and techniques. After reading through everything, you can comb the individual chapters within these sections to pick and choose the best techniques for your own personal use.

BUILDING YOUR FOUNDATION

CHAPTER ONE

HOW TO IMPRESS YOUR BOSS WITH SEO
ROBBIE WILLIAMS

*"Reworking your resume to put key words from the job description gives you a **one in twenty five** shot as opposed to a **one in six hundred shot.**"*
Craig Yakelis, HR Ryan Seacrest Productions
Previous: HR CBS Television

T he art of being discovered in a digital world can take many different shapes and forms. A person looking to be discovered for their musical talent uses YouTube to share their music videos with the world. An Italian restaurant wanting to be the first listing on Yelp whenever someone looks for Italian asks customers to review them. And with our next interviewee, we found someone hoping to be at the top of the LinkedIn results when recruiters search for candidates.

Let us introduce Robbie Williams. A native of Indianapolis, Indiana, it wasn't too long ago that he enrolled in Ball State

University strictly because he wanted to party and have fun. He ended up failing out of school twice within the two years that followed, and ultimately dropped out. Realizing that there's more to life than frat parties, Robbie wanted to get back on track so he enrolled in a local community college. There he earned a 4.0 GPA, good enough to transfer to Butler University and finish up his communications degree.

It took 5 years, and 4 straight 19+ credit semesters at Butler, but Robbie graduated with a 3.6 GPA, marks which should have been good enough to land a competitive job, right? Robbie thought so too, but it didn't happen. He ended up working a local job that wasn't where he saw himself upon graduation. In other words, he was "underemployed", which as of late 2012 was the case for more than 44% of all recent college grads!

However, as luck would have it, this job allowed him to work with an SEO (Search Engine Optimization) firm, which got him thinking, "Why not SEO?"

With a hunch of where he could see himself heading, Robbie decided to start applying to a number of SEO jobs within the marketplace. Not unlike the popular practice of treating job applications like a contact sport, Robbie applied and applied without a response. That's when Robbie realized: He needed to use the very skills his target companies were looking for in order to make himself stand out. He needed to SEO his LinkedIn profile so that SEO firms could more easily find him.

The underlying principles of SEO are simple. The better and more relevant your content is, the more likely a search engine like Google or LinkedIn's internal search can find it. LinkedIn is nothing more than a search engine straddling content, and in this case the content is a slew of professional profiles.

Instead of reinventing the wheel, Robbie leveraged all of the content that was meticulously thought out for the position he wanted. For example, Robbie wanted to work in SEO, so he collected SEO job postings and tailored his LinkedIn experiences to include those very words; words that would then be used by the hiring company when looking for the right people to hire.

Well wouldn't you know that by SEO-ing his LinkedIn, targeting the same SEO companies he once applied for previously, Robbie's luck started to change. Those very same companies were now contacting Robbie! And think about this: Applying the same techniques he'd be expected to use if hired made for a *great* interview. When asked the inevitable question of "What qualifies you for a position in SEO?", Robbie can easily explain his story of targeting that very company and doing it well enough that *they* came to *him*. Needless to say, Robbie got his start at the company he had wanted all along. Now only a few short years later, Robbie is a director at an SEO firm, all resulting from executing this strategy the right way early on.

The concept is simple, and the execution isn't rocket science. If it sounds complicated, think about it this way. What are some ways that you've made strong connections and impressed a boss or a boyfriend/girlfriend? You play to what they like. For example, your boss is impressed by a shirt and tie, so you wear a shirt and tie and make sure you shine your shoes too. Or if you're dating someone who likes to be surprised, what do you do? You surprise them. This is no different. Companies are looking for talent using certain words within a search engine (LinkedIn), so you arrange your profile to include those very keywords.

Whether you're in the market for a job now, or want to always be found rather than having to one day do the searching, SEO-ing your LinkedIn is a MUST. Any professional who plans on being employed in the future should do this. Get started now by using our breakdown below to help you out!

SEO Breakdown
Prep:

1. Figure out the industry in which you are interested in working. In this example we are going to say Marketing.
2. From there, find a job for which you would like to apply. Do research! Don't just apply for every job you see. Do research on the company, and figure out exactly why you are applying for the job.
   a. In this example, we found a "Business Development & Marketing Coordinator" position that looks interesting.
3. Go through the Objective of Role, Responsibilities, and Skills of the open position.

4. Make a list of all keywords from job description.

   a. For example, the keywords we found were the following: planning, implementation of department activities, social media marketing, inter and intra-departmental relationships, team environment, and outgoing.

You are now ready to SEO your LinkedIn profile:

1. First thing's first! Get on LinkedIn.com if you haven't already. Go to "Edit My Profile" and clean up your "Public Profile Link". If you haven't set up your link yet, click "edit" and change LinkedIn's default URL to a URL with your personal name or something close to it.

2. You want to optimize your "Website Links". You can have up to 3 links, and you want to use them all! They appear in your public profile, and they pass SEO authority.

   a. For one of our links, we optimized by saying, "Undertone (company name)—Business Development (keyword)"

   b. For the second, we said, "Bookzingo (name of website Mel started)—Social Media (keyword)"

3. Next, click the "Edit" button by "Summary". Use your "Summary" section to input keywords from the job description in a way that flows naturally.

4. Edit your "Experience" and "Skills and Expertise" sections to fit as many keywords as you possibly can. At the same time, make sure it does not look forced.

5. The groups you are in are very important and play a big role in the SEO of your LinkedIn Profile. In order to search

for groups select "Groups" in the heading and type in a keyword.

6. Take a look at the groups, and if there are some you would like to join, click "select group".

   a. One of our keywords was "social media marketing", so we joined the Social Media Marketing group.

CHAPTER TWO

PREZI IS THE NEW FACEBOOK
ALIZA RABINOWITZ

Like many college students, Aliza didn't begin seriously thinking about the job hunt until the second semester of her senior year at Quinnipiac. Despite multiple marketing internships, Aliza was not passionate about any of these companies, so she decided to start fresh. In the first month of the search, Aliza and her friends applied to jobs via LinkedIn and Mediabistro postings, but heard nothing back. Quickly she realized this wasn't working, so she decided to change it up.

In Aliza's second round of applications, she began to craft what she calls "strange" cover letters that were **bold** and more eye-catching than your standard letter. One example that got the best response was her letter that began with a simple, "Dear Mr. Smith, I'm hungry." She continued the letter to include things such as, "I'm hungry for opportunities to apply the communications skills I've learned throughout college in order to...", but that was fluff. That first line of "I'm hungry" was enough to wake some HR managers up and respond to Aliza's application. However, though she got a few responses, they weren't immediate offers to interview. There was still a waiting game while the HR managers pushed her resume into the rest of the stack.

At this point frustration really began to sink in, and Aliza knew that she needed to continue on this vein of "changing it up", but this time take it to a new level. She did extensive research on creative and interesting resumes and was inspired to take one idea, the Facebook resume, and make it her own.

By way of a class project, Aliza had discovered Prezi, which is a presentation tool that allows you to zoom in on specific areas in order to better show a process or flow of a storyboard. It's also a much more interactive presentation than PowerPoint, and it can be shared and viewed by a simple URL. Aliza decided to combine her research and resources in order to make a Facebook resume into a Prezi presentation. Here's a sneak peak:

You can see our step-by-step breakdown of the process Aliza took at the end of this chapter, but here is a quick summary. Aliza began by deconstructing her resume and reformatting it to fit the layout of a Facebook page; references on the left hand side with pictures of the person, work experience in the center with company logos, and activities/honors/skills on the right. She then copied and pasted those sections of the resume onto a screenshot of her Facebook profile page, and put it all onto a PowerPoint slide. Using Prezi, Aliza was able to upload that slide and create an experience that took the viewer through her resume in order to show exactly why she is the best fit for the job. You can see her full resume here: Aliza's Prezi Facebook Resume.

The layout of the Facebook resume and the creation of the Prezi presentation took quite a few late nights, but her investment paid dividends. Aliza sent the presentation link to 3 companies, and the response was astounding. All three companies responded almost immediately to Aliza's emails. Check out one of the emails she received *ten minutes* after sending the Prezi resume:

Aliza used this resume to land herself *two* jobs. The response from HR at the first job that she accepted was positive to the point that HR sent the resume around to the whole company. The sales manager got a hold of it and insisted that Prezi be incorporated into their sales pitches. When she was ready for a new position, Aliza sent out an updated Prezi Facebook resume and landed her second job with the technique. That company had a similar reaction and requested that Aliza give Prezi tutorials to various colleagues so they could incorporate it into their workflow.

Sound too good to be true, or like it must be a difficult task to generate such results? Think again. We had never used Prezi before, so we're providing you with a step-by-step guide of how Prezi works. Get creative and think beyond Facebook. What else would be eye-catching, and what would make sense for the type of companies where you'd like to work? Would a LinkedIn resume be more suitable for a job in corporate finance? Would a Pinterest profile with pictures of your work make more sense for a graphic design position? Should you add a video to demonstrate your speaking abilities for a role in PR? Have fun with this and make it truly yours. Then head to www.boldjobbook.com to show us what you've built and discuss your successes (and failures).

Prezi Breakdown

1. Prezi is a cloud-based presentation software that combines concept maps, posters, and presentations all into one integrated unit. It allows you to create a clean, non-linear presentation where you can zoom in and out of a visual map.
2. Start off by going to www.prezi.com where you can sign up for a free account.
3. Select "New Prezi", provide a title, and choose a canvas style. Click "Create".
4. You now have the option to select a template. The templates are visual metaphors for your ideas.
5. Once you have selected a template or gone with the blank canvas, it is time to add content.

Prezi can feel a little intimidating until you get the hang of it. Everything is different depending on what you want to do. But, let's say you want to upload a PowerPoint presentation for resume purposes like Aliza.

6. Select "PowerPoint" in the upper right-hand corner
   a. "Open" the PowerPoint you would like to upload
      On the right side bar, you will see that Prezi automatically converts and inserts your slides
   b. Drag your slides one at a time onto the canvas or insert all of them
   c. Select an automatic layout for your slides and select whether or not you would like a path automatically added.
   d. Click "Insert"
   e. Click "Present" to see what your Prezi looks like!
7. Here are a few links to tutorials that will help with any other questions
   http://prezi.com/learn/
   http://www.passyworld.com/passyPDFs/HowToPrezi.pdf
   http://www.youtube.com/watch?v=MAUzEEJ8x3c

CHAPTER THREE

A RED LEGO FISH ATE MY RESUME
KENDRA WIIG

For Kendra, her sights were set on one particular company, an online gaming tech firm that had an opening for a creative problem solving position. Knowing that the traditional route for applying to jobs had not worked for her in the past, she wanted to make sure she displayed her skills in a unique way to stand out. In Kendra's own words: "If you are talented and you are skilled, and you have all of this great stuff to show, but you can't get a human being's eyeballs who can make that decision to read your resume, you aren't going to make it." In today's job market, it's more likely that a robot will read your resume before a human does. Kendra wanted to bypass that robot and ensure that her resume made it into the actual hands of the hiring managers at this company.

Knowing full well that she had no "in" at this company (no friends, LinkedIn connections, etc.), she had to come up with a new way to develop a personal connection with the employees. Kendra's technique revolved around perfecting a resume delivery method that was sure to stand out and display the talents that qualified her for the job. The company sought a creative problem solver, so she needed to show that she could create a positive and entertaining experience for the game players.

How did she do this? After extensively researching the company, Kendra decided to build a giant LEGO sculpture of the company's logo: a red fish with open jaws. She also built a LEGO scuba diver to place her resume into the fish's jaws:

This method demonstrated her in-depth knowledge of the company: She had discovered that the gaming company was in the process of developing an interactive LEGO game.

Kendra recommends that whatever you do, you should incorporate something that you have learned about the firm. For example, Kendra shared another story of someone who was applying for an office manager position and sent his resume on a pizza box after learning about the hiring manager's favorite pizza.

Going with this method also gives you something to discuss in the future. Though Kendra didn't get the job, she was able to leverage the project by showing her creativity to other hiring managers. Also, even if you don't get the specific position for which you applied, you now have a connection with someone at the company for future open jobs. Kendra received a personal email about her LEGO creation from the company, so she now had an inside contact.

Now that Kendra has landed a different job, she's been asked to hire and review resumes. She sees all of the mistakes she once made and wishes she could help everyone abandon the technique of creating template resumes learned in college. In her own words, she wants people to "Start to think about job hunting as a marketing exercise rather than an exercise of filling out checkboxes." Hopefully this story has helped you do just that!

Delivery Method Breakdown

Kendra's example of how she sent her resume with a homemade LEGO structure representing the company mascot is just one example of sending something with your resume in order to get noticed. The idea behind this is simple. Companies get so many resumes that it is so easy to go unnoticed. If you choose to send a paper resume, your hope is that a human being might look at it. Everyone is busy and everyone is stressed, so here is your chance to "wow" someone and brighten his or her day, all the while getting much-needed attention on your resume.

We are not recommending that you send your resume with a box of chocolates. This technique needs to be much more strategic. You are not trying to give a gift to the person reading your resume. You are showing them that you did your research and that you are passionate about getting the job.

Here are the steps to sending something with your resume to get noticed:

1. **Find a company where you would LOVE to work.**
2. **Do your research.** Find something unique to the company, or even better, the person receiving your resume. For example, Kendra's friend found out that every Friday the company he was sending his resume to ordered a pepperoni and sausage pizza. Who knows how he found that out?! But he had his resume sent on Friday with a pepperoni and sausage pizza.
3. **Build, bake, and order away!** Once you have your unique information, come up with the perfect delivery method and send your resume with it. This does not have to be expensive! Just make sure it is well thought out and creative. The goal is to get someone's attention in a positive way and to get your resume read.

CHAPTER FOUR

NEVER JUDGE A SLIDE BY IT'S COVER
EMILAND DE CUBBER

*"I realized the importance of having a story today is
what really separates companies. People don't just wear
our shoes, they tell our story."*

Blake Mycoskie
Founder & CEO of Tom's Shoes

While you may not be in the shoe business, you represent the company of you. You are your own brand, and that brand is what gets you hired. This idea can be broken down in a number of ways, but simply put, your brand represents who, what, where, when, and why you do what you do. Everything from your personal image to the life stories and experiences within your resume should say, "I'm a great person. You should hire me."

At this point, you're probably thinking to yourself, "I have a resume that tells the story of me, what's your angle?" Well for starters, no angle here. We congratulate you for having a resume, but then again everyone else has a resume too. And since you've made it this far into the book, you understand that every technique and idea we're arming you with focuses on one single mission: getting you to stand out from the crowd.

Business Insider did a great article titled "The 500-Year Evolution of the Resume" written by Dona Collins (blogger and writer for CreditLoan.com). We recommend that you read the full article by visiting this link http://read.bi/144aGl5, but since we know you're busy, let us quickly summarize.

In 1482, Leonardo DaVinci wrote the first professional resume, which was followed by a traveling lord in England who offered a handwritten introduction about himself, calling it his resume. Fast forward nearly 500 years, and we still have the same black and white resume that has been tapered down over the years to say the following:

> "Hi, my name is John Doe. I went to this school, and I've had a job or several before. I'm proficient in Microsoft Office products (even though you know that you can only use MS Word and maybe the basics in MS Excel). By the way, here are three to four bullet points summarizing months if not years of experience for each job. Did I mention that I single-handedly grew sales by 500% at my last gig?"

Awesome, you've done something great but we cannot say this enough: so has everyone else. The strategy that we're focusing on in this chapter looks at two things.

First, we want you to turn your resume into a story, and second we want you to make your story **sexy**.

In the first part, we will show you how to write the story using what you already have in your resume, LinkedIn, etc., and in the second, we'll bring it to life with some color so that your story is enjoyable and impressive to read.

It's funny, growing up you were probably taught the phrase, "Never judge a book by its cover." In the job market, you are the book and whatever resume you give to a potential employer is your cover, and guess what. You're being judged entirely by that cover. So we are going to help your cover look sexy, because image is everything when you're one among thousands.

To further put this in perspective, if you've ever gone out for a night on the town, did you dress up? Yes, because you want to stand out. So why are we continuing to use a black and white standard resume format when selling ourselves to potential employers? Let's be honest, that's the equivalent of wearing black funeral attire to your prom. You'll quietly fade into the background.

We could keep the analogies flowing on why image is key, but in the interest of time and giving you the tools to land an awesome job, we'll move on.

When we first had the idea to share a story about someone who embodied this, we synced up with Frenchman Emiland De Cubber. We had heard about Emiland via Slideshare's top presentation of the day (www.slideshare.net/EmilandDC/how-i-landed-a-job-with-slideshare) and reached out to him asking if he'd share his story.

Before we dive in, here's a little background for those of you who may not have heard of Emiland. A young professional, it wasn't too long ago that he was getting ready to graduate from HEC Paris (Europe's #1 ranked business school) and was looking for a job. Prior to this, he had studied at several other universities, transitioning his focus from science to business, while dabbling in a few innovation projects along the way. One of these side projects was as a freelance presentation designer. Interesting.

Trying to avoid fitting his unique story into the structured frame of a resume, he decided to literally build his story using visuals and minimal text. No different than a storybook, Emiland played to his strengths and decided to make this happen in PowerPoint. Check out the below screenshots for a taste of Emiland's quirky and informative presentation.

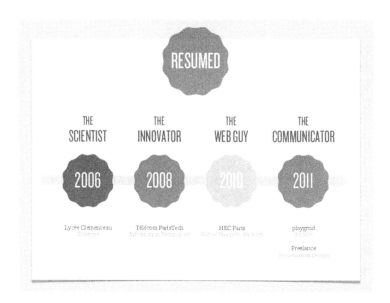

Taking this finished presentation, which mapped out his professional journey to the present day, he uploaded it to Slideshare. com, a popular site where users can share presentations. The beauty in this is that Emiland could simply circulate the link to the companies where he wanted to interview. In this case, the company was TigerLily, a social media agency.

If you decide to follow this straightforward approach, wouldn't it be great if you could tell whether or not your story is being viewed and shared, and by whom? Emiland thought it would be too, which is why he used bit.ly, a company that allows links to be shortened and analyzed. Quickly, Emiland used his free account to convert his presentation link from Slideshare.com/... into a trackable link via bit.ly. If you have questions about this, a great resource for a quick tutorial can be found here: http://slidesha.re/102zt5A

As you can see, the above link was shortened using bit.ly, and it connects to a quick "How To Use Bit.ly" guide hosted on Slideshare.

Using his presentation's shortened link, Emiland emailed a handful of people at TigerLily, and within an hour, he saw that his presentation had been viewed more than twenty times (presumably by TigerLily employees). Shortly after this, someone at TigerLily contacted Emiland directly, and the rest is history as he landed the job he wanted.

Cool story right? Why couldn't that happen to you?

While nothing is guaranteed, each of the techniques we address help give you the leg up you need to land the job you want. At the very least, it's a hell of a lot better than blindly sending out resumes, and this story is no different. So get started and follow the guide below to tell you own story.

Slideshare Breakdown

Before you start, you should know that Slideshare is an online hosting service. Users can upload files in the following file formats: PowerPoint, PDF, or OpenOffice*. You would never send a company a PowerPoint of your resume, but you can send them a link to your Slideshare. It's clean and easy. *Note: You cannot upload Keynote files, but you can easily export as a PDF and upload that way.

1. Go to www.slideshare.net.
2. Click "Sign up" in the upper right hand corner and set up your account.
3. Click the orange "Upload" button to upload power point or whatever file you are using.
4. Once you fill in a few things about the presentation, click "Save".
5. Click the small arrow in the upper right hand corner that leads to a drop down menu.
6. Choose "My Uploads".
7. Once you are happy with the presentation you have, you can copy the URL of the page and create a bit.ly. Then send that bit.ly URL to the proper contacts at the company for which you hope to interview.

We found this cool article with a few great resumes on Slideshare. Feel free to check them out here to get those creative juices flowing: http://workawesome.com/career/top-10-powerpoint-resume-presentations-on-slideshare/

If you're into art and any type of creative design, great! You probably already have ideas swirling around in your head. But if you're like the majority of us who are left scratching our heads, don't worry, we have you covered.

As Emiland's successful presentation suggests, you want to segment your story into different "Chapters of Life" starting with the first relevant experience and working your way to present day. Anything you include should of course add value. The folks who are viewing your presentation don't have time for fluff.

For instance, if you were applying for a marketing job, you probably wouldn't mention that summer you spent waiting tables. Unless of course you were doing it to meet with marketing executives that frequented your restaurant, and out of those contacts, one of them offered you a marketing internship the following year. If your examples help drive your story, then include it, but if it leads to a dead end, or you can't find a bridge into your end goal, it's best to leave it out.

When it comes to making your story look sexy in PowerPoint, you may not know how to pull that off, but we're 100% positive someone else does. If you're in a bind and want to spend money, you can probably find a presentation designer by searching Google, but our book isn't about offering solutions that will take money out of your pocket. Instead, go to Slideshare.net and view a few presentations that you think look sharp. Within each presentation, there should be an author or creator listed beneath the presentation title, or at the very least within the presentation itself at the beginning or end. Found them? Now it's your turn to get in touch and ask for help. Whether you use their email address, tweet at them, or contact them via LinkedIn, reach out and say something along the lines of the following note:

> *"Dear FIRST NAME,*
>
> *I just checked out your awesome PRESENTATION NAME presentation via Slideshare. I learned a lot from it, and it looked great! There were a couple of quick design questions that I had. Would you be able to give me 15 minutes on Skype or over the phone to discuss these?*
>
> *Regards,*
> YOUR NAME"

When you speak with them, tell them you're trying to make a creative presentation about yourself and are looking for some quick tips. Heck, you might even be able to get some help designing it directly from them. Like everything, if you want to do something, you need to get out there and do it, so if you're not a designer, go find one. Fortunately, we live in 2013 where everyone and everything is online, so finding someone that can do this for you or help you do it yourself isn't hard.

Best of all, this process not only sells who you are and what you've done, but it shows Company X that you're not just applying to apply but are actually very serious, which is why you've invested personal time and resources to stand out. Pretty powerful stuff, eh?

Additionally, the story you can tell your future employer about how you created your visual presentation will definitely go a long way. Why? Because it's different, and it's cool. Aren't you a cool, innovative person that the company you want to work for should hire?

To recap, this is a very straightforward technique so don't over-complicate it. Your story should read as though you're giving an interviewer a 45-second verbal pitch of yourself. Keep it conversational. The content you'll be using for your story should come directly from your resume, but be sure to focus on the high-level ideas and leave the detail for a future conversation. Don't rush this. Rome wasn't built in a day, and while your presentation probably could be built that quickly, take a few days to reflect and make sure it's the best it can be (note: Emiland recommends roughly one week).

So while the focus right now is on getting you a job, this mantra can and should be applied to everything else you're involved with. Remember, anything that you do is a reflection of your brand and being able to share that in an engaging story will go a lot further than just the typical black and white resume. And when you have your success story from this technique, don't forget to send us an email and let us know!

CHAPTER FIVE

LET YOUR MOUTH DO THE TALKING
VICTOR PETIT

At first glance, Victor Petit's paper resume is by all means a traditional CV in a great layout, with his education and professional experience detailed as you see here:

However, as soon as a hiring manager goes to flip this paper over, a completely interactive experience is born. Check out this video (http://vimeo.com/21228618) and some screenshots to see what we mean:

As you can see in the video, a reader simply scans the QR code that is in place of Victor's mouth on the back of the CV. This opens a YouTube video of Victor's mouth, and there are markings on the resume that show the reader the exact place to sit their smartphone. Once the hiring manager clicks play, Victor's resume comes to life and tells a bit about his background and interests. Immediately, Victor has created a "face-to-face" interaction with the person reviewing his resume, during which he can show his personality, talent, and innovative qualities.

This particular method was perfect for Victor, a communications student looking to make an impact in the advertising world. By combining his learning and passion about improving communication, Victor was able to market his creative problem solving skills and give the hiring manager something to remember.

The main motivation behind this QR code resume was, like most others, to stand out of the pack. Since Victor was still in school in France and looking for an internship, he noticed that his experience and credentials were almost identical to his classmates. As students, no one had much to go on in the way of differentiation, and Victor knew he needed a way to make a lasting impression on anyone who viewed his resume.

Looks complex, doesn't it? On the contrary, this only took Victor about 2 hours to implement once he came up with the idea. He was able to capitalize on the design talent of his friends to ensure the end product would be professional and aesthetically pleasing.

In order to get in front of his dream companies, Victor mailed a hard copy of the QR code resume to hiring managers and followed up via email. He was able to land a digital creative position, working on multiple strategic digital planning projects just as he had hoped.

Victor notes that because he was looking for a job in the creative agency world, this method fit right in and was very well received. If he had been applying to more conservative and traditional positions, it may not have worked as well. How can you incorporate this into your own job search?

QR Code Talking Resume Breakdown

1. Take a professional picture of yourself that will be placed on the back of your resume. It should take up the full size of your paper resume.
2. Take a video just of your mouth talking. The key is to make sure your mouth in the video is in exact proportion to the photo.
3. When you are talking, you can say anything that you would want the person reading your resume to hear. Be creative!
4. Upload the video you've taken of your mouth to YouTube.
5. There are many different ways you can go about this next step. One easy website you can use to generate the QR code is qrcode.kaywa.com. From there, all you have to do is copy the URL of the YouTube video, and a QR code will be generated.
6. Now you have a QR code! This can be copied and pasted to your resume for immediate use.
7. Now you must make a few markings on your resume so whoever is looking at your resume knows where to scan the QR code and place their phone.
8. Send away your hard copies, and be sure to follow up in a couple days via email. Good luck!

CHAPTER SIX

WHAT COULD I DO FOR YOU?

ALICE LEE

"Show me results, and show it to me well."

Richard Hudock

HR Coca-Cola

Advice from Rich at Coca-Cola

Those who are fresh out of college looking for a job, you are competing with your graduating class, the previous two graduating classes, and those who have been laid off. Everyone is fighting for that entry-level position. It is all about separating yourself from your competition. One way to separate yourself is in your resume and cover letter. I do not want to know what you did; I want to know the RESULTS.

Alice Lee, a recent graduate from the University of Pennsylvania, had her heart set on getting a design and development internship at the wildly famous photo app company, Instagram. But there was one catch—Alice was a business student, not design. Though she had a wealth of experience from high caliber internships with Microsoft and foursquare, she was sure that the skills on her resume wouldn't be enough to land this job. In order to prove her passion and show that she had what it took to transition to design, she did what seemed like the most direct approach in her mind: design and code an open letter to Instagram.

By designing beautiful graphics and telling explicitly how she would add value at Instagram, Alice created a way to show her skills and offer immediately actionable ideas. She clearly labeled these contributions as "What I could do for you", so there was nothing left for the Instagram team to imagine. Check out the full site here, as well as some screenshots below:
http://dearinstagram.byalicelee.com/

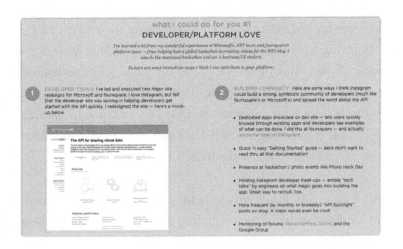

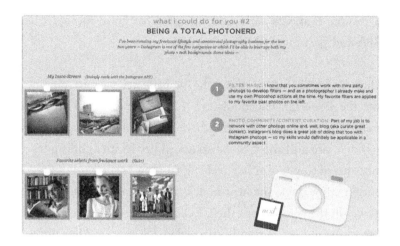

Using her creativity, she was able to get across another incredibly important quality of hers. Alice's passion for photography, Instagram, and design was prominently on display. Tradition-

37

al resume elements were also included for good measure, like GPA and past internship experience.

Alice slowly began posting the website to various channels like the Penn CS Facebook group, her personal Twitter, and eventually to Hacker News, where numerous publications ran with her site and story. She also asked her former colleagues at foursquare to pass on her website to their Instagram contacts. Within a few days, she heard back from Instagram and actually spoke on the phone with the CEO. Alice's goal was to get their attention, and she certainly succeeded. Ultimately Alice did not get a job at Instagram, but of course, other great companies took notice of Alice's skill, drive, and passion. Plenty of firms reached out to Alice, one of the first being Path, a social network widely based around photos, actions, and events. She was offered (and enthusiastically accepted) an internship with Path.

Though she didn't get the job at Instagram, Alice was not disappointed at all. Her advice for someone attempting an approach like this is as follows: "Don't take yourself too seriously, but work really *really* hard. Show your passion, but don't expect people to owe you anything just because you're putting yourself out there." It takes a lot of courage to take a risk like this, and an equal amount to not get down on yourself if it doesn't work out. Alice also mentioned that even if you don't have design or technical skills, there's always something unique and interesting you can do to apply for a job. If you can't think of anything, she thinks it's likely that it's not the right job for you after all.

THE BOB DYLAN APPROACH TO NETWORKING
GRAEME ANTHONY

A side from cute animal videos distracting you during your workday, YouTube can also be used in practical ways to help with DIY projects, learning to play guitar, or even landing you your next job. Graeme Anthony, an Englishman who studied at Leeds Metropolitan University, had everything that the ideal candidate should. He was a hardworking student with good grades and wonderful experience during his years at university. Leeds encouraged communications and marketing students to accept one-day work placements with various companies in order to develop real-world skills. This was huge for Graeme, who, as a result, realized that he wanted to work at a PR agency.

Graeme's degree and experience landed him a job right out of school, but when he made the personal decision to move to London, Graeme was on the job hunt once again. Like most job seekers, Graeme began to write his resume that would then be sent to numerous PR agencies in London. However during this process, Graeme had a realization: "If I'm bored writing my own CV, how bored is my audience going to be?" He also knew that other candidates were going through this same exact process of writing down their experience into a template CV. With so many people doing the same thing, how was he to differentiate himself as an outstanding candidate?

As Graeme mulled over ways that he could distinguish himself from the herd of job seekers, he knew he wanted to get across a few key points: 1. He is a real person, with a personality and social skills; 2. He is qualified, having worked on huge campaigns at his current position as a Senior Account Manager; and 3. His experience is diverse and creative in nature, and he'd like to prove his creativity. With these key points in mind, Graeme came up with an idea to make an interactive video resume to forward to senior members of his favorite PR organizations.

His C.V.I.V (curriculum vitae interactive video) can be seen here. Take a few minutes and pretend you're a hiring manager, reading through piles of boring standard CVs, only to land on this link in an email from Graeme. In the intro video, you learn who Graeme is in thirty seconds—a creative, talented, real individual with a great personality who isn't afraid to be different. You're then instructed to check out other YouTube video links, which you can click on right from the video screen:

Within these other videos (About Me, Portfolio, Skills, Timeline, and Contact), you learn more and more about Graeme and whether or not he'd be a good fit for your company. These videos are simple and provide pretty standard information—the same kinds of facts you would learn by reading Graeme's paper CV—but the way the information is presented is everything here. Our personal favorite is the Skills video, where he uses some movie magic and a Bob Dylan song to spice up a list of capabilities:

(Compare to actual Bob Dylan music video for Subterranean Homesick Blues)

41

This approach not only landed Graeme a job at the agency of his choice (Frank PR), but when that agency encouraged him to go public with the C.V.I.V., numerous publications took note (BBC News, for example). His story was blogged about by famous PR agencies, and eventually went viral. So much so, that at one point, Graeme was the second most searched for person online, falling behind the one and only Justin Bieber.

While this approach worked for him, you'll want to keep one thing in mind. Graeme noted that if he were to apply for another job, he would do something completely different. This technique was right for him at the time, and worked because it was unique. But as the times change, a creative person must also change their approach. Graeme recommends that you always think, "What can you do or say that is absolutely unique?" Additionally, while social media and the Internet can get you in front of people, you still need to have the substance and qualifications to prove you're right for the job.

YouTube Breakdown—How to Link *to* a YouTube Video *from* a YouTube Video

The tools that Graeme used to put together his interactive You-Tube video are actually very user friendly and easy to implement. Plain and simple, he recorded each chapter, and then put "visual links" into the final edits of the chapters.

1. To start off you must create a YouTube account so you are able to upload all of your different videos. You of course can do this from youtube.com.
2. Record your different "Chapters" as different videos.
3. Upload each video separately.
4. Go into "Video Manager" and select "Edit" on the video you plan on having the viewer see first.
5. Select "Annotations" at the top middle section of the page.
6. Select "Add annotation". You can play around with the way you want to add the link, but if you want to do something similar to Graeme then select "Title".
7. Write in the title of the link you want people to click on.
8. Then select "Add annotation" again and select "Spotlight".
9. Drag the spotlight around the "Title" text. Select the "Link" box as an option for the "Spotlight".
10. Here, add the link of the next YouTube video that you would like this particular title to link out to.
11. Repeat this process. You may add as many or as few links as you would like.

TECHNICAL BREAKDOWNS

Using Google Alerts

Google Alert! What is it?

Check it out at www.google.com/alerts. With Google Alerts you can pick specific search terms that Google will monitor for you, and you will get an email when new entries are added to the top search results.

Here are a few things you can use Google Alerts for in your job search:

1. **Research your online reputation**
    Make sure everything on the Internet about you is what you want your interviewers to see. Make sure that all the work you put into the job search doesn't go to waste because Joe Shmoe who is serving prison time has a similar name to you and comes up when someone searches your name. There are ways to fix this!

2. Research new jobs in your location

If you are looking for a job in a certain location, you will get emails when new open jobs fall in the top search results for the location.

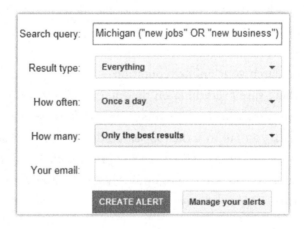

Other ways you can use Google Alerts for your job search are:

- Researching industries
- Researching companies you're interviewing with
- Researching people important to you
- Discovering Key Contacts

Free websites that help keep you organized during the job search!

1. **Evernote**
   Website: evernote.com
   Crash course:
   http://www.youtube.com/watch?v=XjJviCF69GQ
   Slideshare:
   http://www.slideshare.net/teberle/organize-your-job-campaign-with-evernote
   Good for: Keeping your entire job search organized

2. **Jibber Jobber**
   Website: jibberjobberusa.com
   Good for: Tracking and finding jobs, organizing network, and keeping track of companies

3. **Doodle**
   Website: doodle.com
   Good for: Scheduling meetings. Instead of going back and forth 5 times to organize a coffee date, do it all at once.

4. Toodledo
Website: toodledo.com
Good for: Creating to-do lists to increase productivity

How to Write a LinkedIn Invitation

1. **Put yourself in their shoes**
Believe it or not, even the most successful people have had to cold call people for help, so just get to the point and be **honest**.

2. **How did you find them?**
Everyone loves flattery right? Tell the person how you found them. Was it a blog post they wrote, something on their LinkedIn, or something cool they have done? Let them know!

3. **Find a way to relate**
No one likes to help a complete stranger hoping to use him or her as a stepping-stone. Would you? Whether it is a hometown, a common interest, or a favorite sports team, find a way to relate to the person.

4. **They should feel your passion**
This may be a cold email, and the person reading may know nothing about you, but everyone can sense passion. Let the person feel your passion.

5. **They owe you nothing**

   The second you ask them for something, you are done. Don't ask for a job, an interview, or an introduction right off the bat. You need to ease into that in person or over the phone.

6. **It's all about them**

   The only thing you can ask for is 5 minutes of their time with the point being to talk about them. You want to know more about them and their accomplishments. Everyone can stand to talk about themselves for a few minutes.

BEING
DIFFERENT

CHAPTER EIGHT

FINDING YOUR "TRUE NORTH" USING GOOGLE ADS

ALEC BROWNSTEIN

Ordinarily, most people get by in life going from point A to point B by following a very standard path. They go to college, get a job in their field, get promoted, maybe think about getting married, etc. But what happens when a key step, like getting a job for starters, doesn't fall into your lap as easily as expected?

So let's be very real with one another... How far would you go to get the position you want? Think about that for a second.

In this chapter, our interviewee Alec Brownstein wanted to achieve extraordinary results in a field in which he had no experience. Not only was he not qualified, he didn't have a single ounce of related experience to his name that he could sell.

Born in a small suburb outside of Philadelphia, Alec attended Tufts University where he studied International Relations. As he so bluntly put it, he "had absolutely zero job prospects" with a degree in that concentration, and very few major companies were recruiting at his school. This made for a not-so-uncommon predicament that many recent college graduates experience.

Trying to figure out what that next step was after school, Alec sought advice from friends, and one friend in particular suggested advertising. With a radio show at school, and a job writing for a satire magazine, Alec's personality really lent itself to an industry that appreciates the quirky. After looking into the advertising industry further, Alec thought to himself, "Wow, I wish I was doing that." And from there he set a goal to work in advertising.

Thinking he could break into advertising and potentially write some funny commercials, he started contacting anyone and everyone who had an "in" with an ad agency—friend, 4th cousin, the father of friend's girlfriend, whoever. It didn't matter. If they were in the industry and could give Alec the time of day, he was knocking on their door.

As it turned out, every meeting ended nearly the same way with a simple question: "Where's your portfolio?" Having majored in International Relations, Alec clearly didn't have a portfolio of work, and no one was willing to hire him so that he could build one.

Realizing he was in a tough spot, at his last meeting with an ad agency, he decided to scrap the job hunt and offer himself up to the company as an intern so at least he could start building the portfolio everyone wanted to see. As fate would have it, one hour later he got a call from the recruiting manager, who informed him that the company's intern budget had just been slashed, and they wouldn't be able to pay him.

"Fine," said Alec, "Don't pay me."

Another hour shortly after that, the same manager contacted him and said that he would need to take the class for college credit. Having just graduated from Tufts, school was the furthest thing from Alec's mind. Regardless, he replied, "Hang on a second." He immediately got in touch with the community college near his hometown and asked if they had a class offering credit for internships. Luckily, they offered one, and Alec enrolled immediately. Alec started his internship the following week.

During Alec's first week, he walked office-to-office trying to pick up extra work. With nothing to lose, many managers obliged, giving him the shot he desperately wanted. Going one step further, Alec only pursued managers who had a window in their office as he assumed they'd be the only ones who were high enough on the corporate ladder that they could help him get a job.

A little work here, and a little work there, and he had worked himself into a role. He made it! He was in the industry but wanted more. Alec wanted to work with the best of the best in the advertising industry, but in order to do so, he had to know where the best of the best was. This is important as it gave Alec a "true north" to focus on during the job search journey, rather than just saying, "I want to work in business." Alec's advice on this is to be as specific as possible, just like him.

Creating his "true north," Alec narrowed his search down to five advertising agencies, and more specifically, five creative directors for whom he wanted to work. His challenge now was to find a creative means to reach out to these directors and say, "Hire me. I'm good at this advertising stuff. Yeah, lots of people have portfolios, but you should really pay attention to mine."

One day when *googling* himself, the "it" idea hit him. Certainly everyone Googles their own name, as people are generally curious to know what's out there about themselves. You've done this before right?

With that insight in mind, Alec figured if he could get in front of the creative directors at that particular, private moment when they're vainly searching for themselves, he might be able to make an impression. If he could do this, then suddenly the massive amounts of competition in this industry would no longer matter.

Alec wasn't competing with anyone but himself for ad space on Google. So Alec set about purchasing Google Ads targeting those five recruiters. Now, when one of the creative directors googled his or her own name, an ad for (and from) Alec popped up. The ads read something like this:

"Hey, <<creative director's name>>, Googling yourself is a lot of fun. Hiring me is fun, too: alecbrownstein.com."

Of the five creative directors advertised to, four of them gave him an interview. From the four interviews, Alec received two job offers, which ultimately led to him working at Y&R New York.

Total cost of this technique: $6 in Google ads.

It's funny too because each person that contacted Alec always had the same intro: "Well, someone was Googling me and came across your ad." Not trying to be a jerk, Alec breezed passed this detail, and in reflecting back on this experience shared that this ad trick wasn't what got him the job. Everyone who viewed his portfolio actually liked what he or she saw. However, without this personal search advertisement campaign, Alec's resume would never have risen up through the pile like it did.

This technique is easily replicable following these few steps:

1. Watch this video for instructions before you begin: https://www.youtube.com/watch?v=tx2L6EGa9DY&feature=player_embedded
2. Go to adwords.google.com
3. There are 4 main steps to creating an adword campaign:
   a. Choose your budget
   b. Create your ads

    c. Select keywords that match your ads to potential cus-
       tomers

    d. Enter your billing information

While Alec's story focuses on determination and put an insight into action using Google advertisements, you should remember that he did *something*. His technique wasn't proven, it wasn't flashy, and it wasn't conventional by any means. He just did *something*, took the chance of being embarrassed as the worst-case scenario, and he eventually reaped the rewards.

For more information about Alec's story, please visit
http://www.youtube.com/watch?v=7FRwCs99DWg

CHAPTER NINE

MAKE IT HARD FOR YOUR EMPLOYER TO SAY "NO!"

LIZ TAUB

There is someone who you want to contact. You think they're larger than life and completely unapproachable. In reality most people are reachable. We've spoken with Elizabeth Taub to demystify the process of contacting big names.

Getting on the phone with Liz was nearly impossible. To say her schedule is hectic and action-packed would be an understatement. A proud employee of Walgreens (corporate office), she heads a training program called REDI (Retail Employees Distribution Initiative). After several back and forth email exchanges, she was able to squeeze us in for a chat following a meeting with one of the Senior Vice Presidents at Walgreens.

Graduating just a few years back in 2011, Liz was fresh out of New York University and passionate about doing something that would give back, like social work. Even with a degree from a reputable University like NYU, Liz, like everyone else, was excited just to land her first job. She started out with a company called HOAP (Homeless Outreach and Advocacy Program).

While there she realized social work was not everything she had always imagined. Liz quickly came to the realization that she could not change lives over night, and blood, sweat, and tears were part of the job description.

Her passion for social work remained, but she wanted more. Or maybe her consciousness for wanting something else stemmed from the fact that one of her co-workers was badly injured at the homeless shelter she was working at as a result of poor security. She needed to get out...quickly.

While attending an industry conference, Liz was mesmerized by the keynote speaker, Randy Lewis. His business model for training people with disabilities made sense. It was scalable, which was something she had never seen before. Liz watched as people rushed to Randy after his speech and she remembered thinking, "I am a girl who doesn't even have a social work degree. Why would this guy want anything to do with me?" Understanding she'd probably only get one shot at making a good impression, she bit the bullet and joined the crowd competing for their two minutes with Randy.

Pulling herself together, Liz walked up to Randy and said, "Hi, my name is Liz. I am in graduate school for social work at NYU. I want to work for you. **I will pay you** to let me work for you for the summer." Now that's what we call being bold!

His jaw dropped, and he started laughing. As an SVP for Walgreens he had seen a lot, but never this. He handed Liz his business card and said, "Email me your resume. I am sure we can work out a better deal."

Thinking that Randy was just being nice in giving her his card, Liz was sure she was a small fish in the sea of people trying to sync up, but she'd never know until she tried. And when she tried, she'd have to stand out.

While contemplating what to say in her email, Liz recalled one of the questions posed to Randy at the conference: "How can we get more people with disabilities working for us?" Randy replied, "Make it hard for the employer to say no." These words resonated loud and clear as Liz drafted her follow-up. Though originally structured around the disability employment discussion, this advice could be her differentiator to jump off the screen in her email.

Liz began writing. "You said to make it hard for the employer to say no, so this is me taking your advice." What Liz wrote in the rest of the email could have been in another language; it didn't matter. Randy was sold.

The rest is history as they say. Liz landed her dream internship with Randy, and upon graduating from NYU, a full-time position at Walgreens opened up which she gladly accepted.

This "technique" is so simple, and yet it worked because it's genuine. Elizabeth had passion, she made that passion known to those who mattered, and she focused on delivering a quality, tailored communication that would resonate with her target. As we've been instilling in each of these chapters, casting the widest net possible isn't going to do you any favors. Rather, determine what you want, spend the time doing it right, and get it done.

CHAPTER TEN

DESIGNED TO BE A HUSTLER
MARISSA SAUER

Meet Marissa, a young professional in her mid-twenties living in Hoboken, NJ, as the owner of her own design company. She's worked on numerous television shows as design coordinator and head designer. And she never went to design school. How did Marissa make this all happen? She's a tried-and-true hustler.

Marissa knew she wanted to work in TV, but it wasn't until the last minute during college that she realized she wanted to work in design specifically. Typically, to get any design job in TV production, a design degree would be required. But Marissa found a way to get her foot in the door and work her way up, gaining incredible experience along the way.

Craigslist

Marissa realized that employers who post on Craigslist tend to need someone right away, and will almost always respond to your inquiry—and she swears it's not creepy. In fact, about 90% of Marissa's jobs have been found this way. Her very first job out of school was an internship listing found on Craigslist (by her mother, no less), and it led to a three-year stint with an incredibly reputable design TV show, Dear Genevieve. But she still had to hustle to get this.

The Hustle

The interviewer was confused as to why Marissa, who had plenty of internship experience and was working a full-time paying job, would want to take another internship. She had to work to convince the employer that she wanted *this* internship, because she knew that design production was what she wanted to do for the rest of her life and she would take an internship to get her foot in the door and prove herself and her work. The interviewer appreciated Marissa's confidence and passion, and gave Marissa the internship. She worked her way up the ladder to design coordinator and eventually became the Head Designer for a brand new TV show, Mancaves.

This isn't the only time Marissa used her determination to get in front of decision makers. During college, once she had her sights set on working in design, Marissa TiVo'd every design show and paused the show during the credits to identify the production companies involved. She then searched for every company on both Google and LinkedIn, and reached out to every person she could find located near her school in D.C.

Marissa called, emailed, and sent her resume out regardless of whether or not there were internship and/or job openings.

Though many doors slammed in her face, she experienced success and landed an internship that allowed her to experience both the design and production side of things so that she could zero in on exactly what she wanted to do.

Still hustling?

Today, as the sole owner of her design company, Marissa's work (and income) revolves around landing freelance jobs constantly. She continues to use Craigslist to search for her next job and sends out 5-10 emails a week trying to get hired. When she does get a bite back from one of those contacts, she focuses all her energy on landing an interview and the job. Her advice when looking for work is this: "Every five people that I reach out to, I get one interview. You can't expect that every company is going to call you back. You can't expect that every company you think is perfect is going to be perfect. You can't expect that everywhere you want to work is going to want to work with you!"

Craigslist Breakdown

Craigslist is a great resource because companies will put up a job if they are looking for something quick. Marissa, who works in interior design and entertainment, still finds the majority of her jobs through Craigslist. Companies have to pay to post a job, so they actually do take it seriously.

1. Go to Craigslist.org.
2. Click into the city you are looking to find a job.

3. Under "Jobs" click on the industry you wish to work in. For example, we chose "marketing/PR/ad".

4. You will find jobs listed by most recent post. There may not be many jobs for what you are looking for, but make it a habit to check Craigslist every day just to see if something pops up.

5. Email the poster with your contact information and a little about yourself. Tell them your phone number and email so they can contact you for more information and your resume. Don't give it all away in the email, or they may choose to skip over you. Leave them wanting more so that they have to call you. (No, we're not talking about dating, but same rules apply!) Or better yet, if there's a phone number, call! We live in such a digital age now that email is expected, and we tend to forget that hiring managers still have a phone on their desk. Getting a phone call will be a pleasant surprise, and may be just what you need to get hired!

CHAPTER ELEVEN

REJECTION IS NOT AN OPTION
FLAVIE BAGNOL

"I respect people who are persistent. Be persistent in a pleasant way and not in an annoying way. Dating for example. I am sure you have gone out with a guy who has been persistent, but others are just found annoying. When applying for jobs you have got to work with the numbers. You cannot send out three cold emails and get rejected and think you are a failure."

Mike Mabunay
Sr. Director, Account Development at Time Warner Cable

Flavie Bagnol moved to America from France when she was eighteen. When every other kid her age was off to college, Flavie was sitting in the back of a high school classroom, trying to learn a new language. For two years, she battled her way to learning English, all the while figuring out how she was going to survive in the world's most expensive playground: Manhattan.

After two years in the high school classroom, she enrolled in a community college. It was pure focus for Flavie at Westchester Community College. She earned a 4.0 after only two years of speaking the English language and was awarded a Pepsi scholarship to finish her last two years at Hunter College. When reflecting on this time, Flavie told us, "I think that it is very important to look at what is available around you at college, and talk to your professors because they are the ones who know what to do. They have been there and done that."

While in school, Flavie was working part time as an au pair, babysitting on the weekends, and working nights at a restaurant. She was surviving. All she knew was that she wanted to work in TV, and her passion was in communications and broadcasting.

At the high-end restaurant where she worked, a few of her customers were in the TV business, and one specifically was a reporter on the local news station, New York 1. One night, Flavie asked the reporter for an internship. He kindly told her he really just does his own thing and was not looking for an intern. Instead of accepting the rejection, Flavie persisted, saying, "Yes, but I will follow you everywhere and do whatever you need me to do." And with that, her internship started at 8am the next morning.

Her internship consisted of getting coffee, fetching the newspaper, and logging tapes. Eventually she paid her dues, and they started bringing her along on the video shoots. It was at these shoots that she was able to talk and connect with people in the TV industry.

"I would talk to girls who were just a few years older than me and realized it is all about who you know. If you don't start doing the research about who it is you need to know in the industry that you want to work in, young enough, you are going to miss out on that. Hard work is very important, but going to the right people can almost be more important."

During Flavie's senior year, she took a PR class from a man who was working in the industry but still teaching a few classes in the evening. She was given an assignment to pitch a short story to a magazine or newspaper in New York. While most of her classmates were going to the local neighborhood newspapers, Flavie put her pride aside and went right to The New York Times. Her piece was published.

"So then I realized, why just settle for small things. You can go to the top. It is a matter of really wanting it and putting the effort into it. You can just go and do it."

Once Flavie finished college, she knew she wanted to work in current affairs and international news. She looked at two places that seemed to be right for her in terms of her interest: CNN and CBS. She headed to her college career center and found a few contacts from each company. Flavie sent her resume off to every contact she found, and to no one's surprise, she did not hear anything back.

CBS headquarters wasn't far from her house, so Flavie walked into the building and asked the woman working the front desk to pass her resume along to the contact to whom she had addressed her envelope.

The receptionist insisted that Flavie couldn't meet any of the people she was asking about, but after more persistence the woman gave Flavie the name of the person in charge of the CBS Page Program (similar to a paid internship program; think Kenneth from 30 Rock!).

Flavie called the person in charge of this program and left a message, to which there was no reply. She called again, and left another message. On her third call, she finally spoke to someone who told her there were no openings for the page program. However, as was typical for Flavie, she didn't just accept the rejection. Instead, Flavie called back a few times a week to check for an opening. After one month, there was finally an opening... Or maybe they were just sick of getting phone calls from Flavie. Regardless, Flavie had an interview the next morning at 8am.

"I really didn't know anything, but I gave them the best I could give them in terms of my passion for broadcast news and current events. They probably thought, 'She may not know anything, but she wants it.' So one week later I started at 7am working crazy hours."

Flavie's constant persistence and fearlessness have gotten her all the way from having her foot in the door to the top of her industry. As of today, Flavie has worked at CBS and Thrillist, and she now owns her own PR agency. She is easily one of the most powerful and well-known professionals in her industry. No one looks at Flavie and says she should be embarrassed for putting herself out there. In fact, most people are like us, just asking for five minutes of her day.

CHAPTER TWELVE

LIGHTING UP
LIZ HICKOK

"It had long since come to my attention that people of accomplishment rarely sat back and let things happen to them. They went out and happened to things."

Leonardo Da Vinci

et's go back to the fundamentals for a second. The goal here is to land a job, but not just any job—life is too short to have one that doesn't make you happy. You want to land your dream job. For the application process, one has to assume that everyone else out there applying has some form of credentials like a college degree, a few interesting internships or work experiences, and their own story to bring to the discussion table. Additionally, you can assume that everyone who isn't reading this book is continuing to follow the traditional cycle of submitting a resume and writing a follow up email.

During the days of excessive unemployment, and record numbers of college diplomas competing for jobs, "happening to things" and standing out can better position you in your job search. What's even better? Building an army of support behind you.

Before diving into a few of the examples of how to stand out like we detail in most chapters, let's start with a question: Can you think of a recent news story calling for donations, or a challenge that would take place if that user reached a million Facebook likes? Maybe it was just an awareness story about some teenagers and their business or a charity event supporting animal welfare. Not sure what we're talking about? They run stories like this everyday on Yahoo!, AOL, Huffington Post, etc., and the public eats it up. At the end of the day, these are just stories about people with a cause, and more often than not the public throws their support behind them somehow. In a lot of cases, the stories we feature throughout this book have been featured in the biggest news publications and media outlets. Knowing this, we asked everyone we spoke with what this did for their job prospects once they were featured, and not surprisingly, they got the attention of the company they were pursuing, in addition to countless other companies looking to hire them too. All it takes is a little creativity like we've been preaching, and when you add a little publicity, good things happen.

Now that we've set the stage, let's introduce Liz Hickok. A life-long learner, Liz started her career in speech and language pathology before making the leap into Human Resources. After gaining experience in a number of different industries, including a ten-year stint working at a large software company, she became a victim of corporate downsizing. Not unlike many college students or recent graduates looking for their first job, Liz was back to square one looking to start fresh in a market she knew nothing about.

Having never had to really worry about landing a job in today's economy, Liz thought long and hard about what she wanted. Using her recently created LinkedIn profile, she established some leads, but with her approach she wasn't able to generate much traction.

With a background in HR, Liz knew this process would take time, which she accepted. In speaking with her, Liz shared the following rule of thumb:

> "As an *entry-level applicant*, the process can take anywhere from a few weeks to a few months, whereas a seasoned professional can take months to a year to find the *right* job."

Even though she knew this process could take time, she wasn't going to wait for the usual to run its course. Rather, Liz thought it'd be best to approach this from a different angle. Recognizing the need to stand out, she decided she'd take her job search campaign public.

Thanksgiving had just concluded and holiday season was in full swing. With every house around her setting up their Christmas decorations, a chord of inspiration struck Liz.

She lived in a house on a heavily trafficked street and decided that this year her Christmas lights wouldn't be strung over a tree, or around a fake reindeer on her family's front lawn. Instead, she was going to spell out her mission to land a job by stringing her Christmas lights onto a wooden board, and hanging that board on the front of her house for all passersby to see. And see they did.

On what was a busy and fast-paced street, the speed limit suddenly slowed as cars driving by tried to read Liz's message, which read, *"MY WISH—HR JOB. LIZ HICKOK—LINKE-DIN"*. Check out this picture of the lights in actions!

As Liz noticed the volume of traffic nearly coming to a halt in front of her house, she tipped off a neighbor that worked for a local TV station. After her story first aired, channels from across the country including Business Insider, CBS Atlanta, local ABC, and more picked it up.

Shortly after this publicity exploded, Liz received tons of interest and interviews from various companies, one of which resulted in landing her now-current job!

Personal Public Relations Campaign Breakdown

In most chapters we like to take the technique used, break it down for you, and give you the tools to go off and recreate it on your own. And while the ultimate message here is to get your story in front of the public via TV, radio, print, billboards, etc., we're certainly not suggesting you run to your local hardware store and pick up 1000 red lights. Focus instead on what Liz was after, and how she executed.

The bottom line is that you're entirely capable of being the next story featured on the 6 o'clock news, or on the front page of the Sunday paper, or even featured as the main article on Mashable.com. You need to craft your message, and then start a public relations (PR) campaign to share what you're doing. Don't overcomplicate this last step. The best part about this is that media and news outlets are looking for a cool story like yours to feature; you just need to make them aware that you're the next big thing.

Getting out there is easy and we recommend these quick steps:

1. Google the stations or distribution channels (magazine, blog, radio, etc.) that you want to reach.

2. Locate the "Contact Us" or "Submit Story" link.

3. Craft a quick and easy note like the following:

"To whom it may concern,

My name is **INSERT NAME***, and I'm working to land a job in* **INSERT THE FIELD OF WORK** *(e.g.* **Finance***). To support this, I've* **INSERT YOUR JOB CAMPAIGN DE-TAILS** *and have received an overwhelming response from the public.*

To further my efforts while giving **INSERT CHANNEL/ MEDIA NAME** *the opportunity to reflect on the current job market, I'm hoping you can feature my story in an upcoming* **ARTICLE/BROADCAST/ISSUE/ETC***. Any help or support that you can provide would be greatly appreciated.*

Regards,
INSERT NAME"

Getting traction behind your job search efforts isn't rocket science, but it requires you to do something and share that something with the world. You're probably thinking to yourself, "If this is so easy, why isn't everyone doing this?" The answer is simple. This involves thought and creativity and most people (not you) aren't willing to do it. Dropping a resume into a company mailbox is most common because it's easy, it's expected, and it's what everyone else is doing. This method is just as easy, but requires a little creativity, which you have. Before you know it, we'll be hearing about your story.

We're eager to hear from you on your success stories, so please reach out via www.boldjobbook.com to be featured on our website and possibly even a future release of this book!

CHAPTER THIRTEEN

DON'T SWEAT IT, JUST REFORMAT IT!

AVI LICHTSCHEIN

*"If you work really hard, and are kind,
amazing things will happen."*

Conan O'Brien

Getting a job isn't easy. Nobody said it would be. This is hard work, and you will have to work hard. Working smart while working hard, and doing it with the right attitude, as noted by Conan, can pay off, but what's interesting about being in the job market is that it means many different things to many different people. For some, it may mean graduating college and recognizing that moving back in with their parents is not a viable option, so finding a job to cover rent and food becomes a necessity. For others, it may mean keeping their options open to try and find a better deal outside of their current situation. And for almost everyone else, it means finding a lifeline out of unemployment into a job that makes money.

Does one of these scenarios sound like your own situation?

Regardless of your circumstances, knowing where you want to be before you get there is more important now than ever before, particularly regarding which role and at which company.

Talent is everywhere, so in order to stand out, it's imperative that you know what you want.

Imagine the process of getting a job like the process of dating. Typically, you have certain criteria in hopes of finding a suitable match. Time, energy, and in a lot of cases money are all invested in an effort to secure a "second round". Continue playing your cards right, and who knows, you'll likely find yourself in a relationship—a commitment to one another.

None of this is different than finding a job, yet we treat the job hunt like playing the field rather than finding the right match. It's common to hear about current applicants applying to 10, 20, 50+ jobs each month in hopes of landing something. Job-hunting should not be treated as a numbers game. Rather, as is often true, quality will trump quantity. If you're serious about landing the job you know you deserve, your approach needs to be serious too.

To put all of this in context, we spoke with ex-Square & AOL marketing/sales guru, Avi Lichtschein, who brings a whole new meaning to the word hustle. Fresh out of Yeshiva University,

Avi was trying to figure out his next move. He had a brief stint in rabbinical school studying to become a Rabbi, shortly followed by a role as a divorce settlement negotiator for Jewish couples. His background makes for a compelling story so for full detail, be sure to check out our recorded interview with Avi on our website (www.boldjobbook.com).

Despite testing the waters in several different Judaic professions, Avi always had a passion for the tech startup world. Avi stayed updated via the usual suspects like TechCrunch and Mashable, yet kept himself from taking the plunge into the new frontier he knew deep down was where he wanted to be.

At a Phish concert, of all places, he stumbled upon Square. Checking out the t-shirts and band gear at the merchandise table, he noticed the person managing the sales for Phish was swiping credit cards on a device attached to their iPhone. Intrigued, the questions began, and before he knew it he was making connections in his head for how much of an impact this could make. He knew then and there he wanted to be a part of that impact.

Browsing Square's website, Avi saw that there were some small positions at their headquarters. Taking the traditional and easy route, he applied online only to be rejected shortly after. What else is new?

Remember, persistence is key. Getting rejected is normal and is bound to happen even to the best of us. However, getting rejected simply means that single person or single committee didn't find enough immediate synergy between their requirements and the presentation of the information they received. Don't sweat it; just reformat it, and do it well. Down, but not out, Avi knew he had to get Square's attention in the reformat round for his second attempt.

Thinking about what those internal requirements could be, he recognized the business didn't have employees on the ground in his hometown of New York City. Thinking this was a an obvious gap, Avi thought that if he could deliver on that need he would stand a good chance at proving himself and demonstrating value.

So he hired himself into Square.

He used his own money to buy the Square card readers, created his own Square sales materials using publically available information from their website, and hit the sales trail. He went from business to business, signing up customers that would want to use Square for their operation. After a few days of this, he compiled his list of sales leads, put together his story, and sent it back to Square.

The reformat worked. He definitely got their attention to the tune of an offer to work in their "Square U" program. Though Avi was a graduate student being asked to join a program designed for undergraduate students, he jumped at the opportunity. His foot was in the door.

Now we're not suggesting any illegal activities involving you impersonating someone else. (For example, you want to be a police officer so by reading this you rent a police uniform and hit the streets arresting people. Don't do that.) However, Avi's story teaches us that one way to get noticed is to do the following:

1. Identify a need for your target company
2. Figure out a solution for that need
3. Deliver the results back to the company, ideally to someone of authority (see Chapter 18 on finding anyone's email if necessary)

Creativity is great in the form of ideas and hypotheticals, but it's even better when it translates to results. That shows you care enough to put skin in the game with your own time and resources. Not many job seekers are willing to take that risk, but as demonstrated in Avi's story, it can pay off quickly with the desired result.

Let's put this in context and say you're interested in working for a bank as a stockbroker. The easy, but low-result, way would be to write a stock analysis or make a recommendation on what you would do to bring value to the trading team.

The harder yet higher-result and more effective way would be to set up a trading account with your own money (even fake money on one of the trading game sites like Investopedia.com), and put your recommendations into action. Track your results, give it context, and share that story. Win or lose, showing that you understand the company and can put a plan into action addressing their needs will open up more doors than you would imagine.

This doesn't require significant amounts of time or money. Avi was in need of a job, and knew where he wanted to be. He spent less than $250 and no more than a few days creating real value for Square, showing them why he was worth taking a chance on.

Let's assume he makes the national average starting salary for a recent graduate, which is ~$44,928*, which roughly translates to $900/week. Being jobless, Avi's income was zero. If his technique secured him a job one week, three weeks, or even five plus weeks ahead of when he would have secured a job otherwise, his investment pays for itself immediately, many times over.

Spending money during times of uncertainty isn't easy. It takes chutzpa, which is Yiddish for "shameless audacity". But if you want to win and achieve extraordinary results, which in the current climate means landing a job faster than the rest of the pack, you're going to need to demonstrate value, with a bit of chutzpah.

*Source: National Association of Colleges and Employers, "Average Starting Salary for Grads with Bachelors Degree Rises 5.3 Percent," April 17, 2013.

CHAPTER FOURTEEN

HOW NOT TO BE A COLLEGE MASCOT
MATTHEW EPSTEIN

"Your resume will only get you so far. No one buys a car based on the brochure, you have to go into the show room and test it out. Personality, personality, personality."

Mike Mabunay

Sr. Director, Account Development at Time Warner Cable

http://googlepleasehire.me/

Hello Google. My name is Matthew Epstein.
I want to join your product marketing team, bad.

Do you see the guy above, with the perfectly groomed mustache? Looks pretty smart, wouldn't you say? While we like his mustache, we like him even more for his story and technique despite the fact it comes from a guy who says he was "the mascot for what you shouldn't do in college." That started to resonate loud and clear when he shared his success in creating a viral video in which he told Google why he should be hired—all while pants-less and wearing the previously mentioned beautiful (yet fake) mustache.

Throughout college, Matthew Epstein placed a higher value on experiential learning rather than memorizing and regurgitating information in class. Matthew did everything he was supposed to do. Though he "zoned out" most of college, he maintained a 3.5 GPA and landed multiple internships—one every summer in the industry he cared about: advertising. With agency experience under his belt, he was one of the fortunate few to secure a job immediately upon graduation (If only it were that easy for the rest of us!).

But when it came time for a new job four years later, the initial aura and energy around life at the agency waned, and Matthew knew that switching industries was what he needed to do. However, with 4+ years of solid experience under his belt, switching or moving sideways across functions and industries is almost like starting over. As you've heard time and again, most of the people in our book began like everyone else: by sending out resumes and never hearing back, and for Matthew this was no different. Even with a great CV, he didn't get a single response to the few dozen resumes he'd circulated—not even a rejection! At that point, he was just hoping for something, anything. But the reality was in Matthew's case, and the majority of cases today, there are A LOT of qualified people applying for the competitive jobs; and it's easy to get lost, forgotten, or even unseen. Our money's on the latter part, and so was Matthew's, which is why he knew he'd have to go big in order to get seen.

After dealing with his feelings of frustration, he put together a plan. This plan was simple: Spend the next two months on a project about which I'm passionate. The results? This amazing resume targeted at the very company for which he wanted to work, Google: http://googlepleasehire.me/. Take a look.

Now we of course wouldn't recommend that you try to replicate this unique approach. There have been many copycats who just don't seem genuine, and honestly, Google (and millions of other viewers) have already seen this approach. It went viral, remember? What you can take away from this however lies within the approach Matthew took, and the lessons he learned. We broke it down into several prompts that we encourage you to write responses to based on your own experiences.

Knowing what job you want

This particular approach only worked because Matthew knew exactly what type of position he wanted, and what kind of company would be the right fit. Matthew thought through all the companies he was interested in, and pinpointed Google since it had some of the smartest people in the tech field. With his experience and ambition to learn, he knew he wanted to work on the product marketing team. His focused approach was a step above everyone else "testing the market."

Working within your skillset to stand out

Matthew gathered his thoughts, skills, personal quirks, and talent of his videographer friends, and produced what some would call a work of art. If you do the same, you'll come up with something different that will be unique to you and totally badass.

Matthew heard a piece of advice and took it to heart: "When everyone's running one way, you need to run the other way." He thought that no one had done an interview without pants, so he took that idea and ran with it. His personality lent itself to this approach, especially for a product marketing position for which this visual way of marketing himself was the way to go. So think about your ideal job and company, list your skills, and start thinking about an approach that addresses them. Matthew's advice is to stay true to yourself and put work into a project that you truly love, so that regardless of the outcome you'll be proud of what you did.

Do something DIFFERENT!

To put it in perspective, think about the stack of resumes sitting on any HR recruiter's desk. Among the hundreds of resumes, how do you really measure up? Even if you have a great GPA and great college degree, so do most of the other applicants. If you don't have huge company names and ten years of experience on your resume, you need to do something that will shake the pile so that the only remaining resume on the recruiter's desk is yours.

So out with it... did Google hire him?

The short answer is no, Matthew does not work at Google. But he did get an interview and made it through two rounds. His video was good enough to get him noticed and get his foot in the door, which is exactly what this book is about and what you're trying to accomplish. At the end of the day he screwed up a math question and for one reason or another Google didn't see the right fit. So then what?

Rejection

Though he didn't get the job offer, Matthew didn't get down on himself. When he thought about the rejection, he realized that Google didn't reject him because he failed at a project and got fired. He was rejected before he was able to show his marketing talents. The interview process is so quick, and he wasn't able to prove himself during the given time. He failed the interview, but not the job itself. Matthew found it hard to take that personally. Plus, he was proud of the video he made, and Google couldn't take that away from him.

Response from other companies

So he didn't get the job at Google, but he certainly has a job he loves now. Because of the video, he received well over 100 interview requests from companies like Etsy, Amazon, and Microsoft. At the end of the day, he turned down a job with a larger company to work for a startup, and he couldn't be happier with his decision.

CHAPTER FIFTEEN

WORKING LONG HOURS FOR FREE AND PAYING OFF
SCOTT BRITTON

*"As long as the job offers the opportunity to learn
and have valuable experience that is most important."*
Lynn Gaudio, HR Quorum Federal Credit Union
Previous: HR Conde Nast, INC

Y ou look at people who are successful and probably think,
"Gee, that person must be really smart or a product of
a privileged background." Which brings us to Scott Britton. We love Scott's story because yes, he went to Princeton and
he was smart, but his success is not attributed to being gifted
and smart. Scott is a fighter. Through and through, nothing he
has attained has been a given, and he's had to fight tooth and
nail, taking risks left and right to incrementally achieve all that
he has achieved in such a short amount of time.

Scott Britton works in Business Development at Single Plat-
form, has a great blog about personal development (life-long-

learner.com), has written multiple online courses, and is a published author. Oh, and did we mention Scott is only twenty-five years old?

It's no secret, but nearly everyone out there is looking for the quick fix to get everything today, not tomorrow. Let's be very real here: there are no shortcuts, especially in the job market. Scott got traction and success early on because he invested more time and energy in more creative ways than most. Sometimes it works out, sometimes it doesn't, but always remember, if you keep doing the right things over and over again, things tend to sort themselves out because you yourself get them sorted.

Scott graduated from school and moved out to Chicago where he was on the fast-track to becoming a Major League Baseball (MLB) sports agent, representing players and personnel in all of their contracts, negotiations, and professional affairs.

"On the first day of the job, I went to a photo shoot at Victoria Secret with Gordon Beckham who was the 2009 Rookie of the Year for the Chicago White Sox. I was like, this is the sickest job ever." Scott was learning a lot and had some great on-the-job perks, but he still felt like there was something missing.

Less than a year into the job, Scott came across a recently funded start-up in NYC that was founded by one of his classmates, and it caught his attention. Digging into the details, he discovered there was an opening at the company. Living the posh life amongst the rich and famous didn't impress Scott, which is why he took a leap of faith and jumped on the start-up wagon.

He was now an unpaid, Community Manager intern.

"Here I was, captain of the Princeton football team, had good grades, all my friends were getting paid six figures, and I was going to work for free for some random kid and live at my parents' place. Ultimately, it was one of those things I thought I had to do."

During the job search, you will be given advice from everyone about what you should do. Your parents, professors, and friends will steer you towards what they believe to be best. The reality is that each generation and person is different, facing different challenges while pursuing new opportunities. For a long period of time, the employment ideal was to join a corporation, work 25-30 years, and retire with that same company while collecting a decent pension during retirement.

Fast-forward to the current dynamics of the job market. It seems that companies no longer value the lifelong employee clocking in at 9 and punching out at 5, doing the best that they can. It's all about results and delivery today, which means that workers will be brought in or out in the blink of an eye to ensure that results are proven and goals are exceeded. Throw in globalization, technology, and the sheer lust of opportunity on the table, and workers are willing to move much more frequently.

When the right opportunity arrives, we jump at it. That's just what Scott did. Sure, everyone around him thought he was crazy to give up his slot in the highly competitive world of sports agents, which took a wish and a miracle to break into. They thought he was nuts for giving up his paycheck. Scott wasn't taking just a pay cut. He willingly signed up to **work for free** and **work more hours**. Scott did all this in pursuit of an opportunity to get his foot in the door in an industry and company that would fulfill him more than his current, safe situation.

Today, Scott still works every day to continue learning and push forward in his career, but he is at a point far beyond most twenty-five-year-olds in his industry. "Before anything good happened to me I would have told you that I have a really sad story. Today, I feel really fortunate that it has all worked out. It is one of those things that if you keep doing the right things, eventually you will succeed. If you keep networking a ton, providing value to others, working really hard, constantly trying to work and push yourself, eventually if you do enough of those things continuously, something good will happen."

Think about your current situation. Can you draw any similarities? Do you want to be fulfilled in the work you do? How far would you go? It's never too late to take a calculated risk if it will get you to where you want to be. Scott's story doesn't offer you the formula for getting exactly what you want, but it paints a picture of taking control of your path. Understanding what it is you want, and having the courage to take the steps necessary to get that are key. Anything is possible, if you want it badly enough. In today's market, if you have that passion and drive, with a bit of creativity you'll do just fine.

So building on Scott's passion and willingness to go after what he wants, there is an entire book (you're reading it) focused on offering you the techniques and tools to get in front of the right people, the right way, at the company you want. Along the way, you will go out of your comfort zone, you will take some risks, and you will no longer have to deal with the regular garbage everyone else is facing in today's job market.

CREATING
VALUE THROUGH
NETWORKING

CHAPTER SIXTEEN

A DIFFERENT TYPE OF ALUMNI DONATION

TIM DEVANE

"If you know someone, have them help you make a connection. One way someone will get my attention is if someone meaningful at the company puts a resume in front of me. This resume has a sure shot at getting looked at."

Marnie Woodward, HR Bank of America

One of the main reasons we decided to write this book was because we too had been frustrated with the process of getting a job. We were tired of hearing the boring, tactical advice of polish your resume, and drop it off with each company you meet at your school's career fair. Even after we'd spoken to dozens and dozens of people about their creative way to break into the job market, each technique—and all techniques out there for that matter—seem to boil down to one thing: establishing a relationship.

Whether you do something creative with your digital profile (see SEO Your LinkedIn profile—Ch. 1) or you spell out your job story using the Christmas lights on the front of your house (see Liz Hickok's PR Campaign—Ch. 12), everything that you could possibly do to land a job is driven by the relationship you have with the person signing off on your offer letter. This is why the stories we're sharing can have such a big impact; they'll get you to where you want to be that much quicker.

So it should come as no surprise that one of the easiest ways to establish a relationship is to have something in common with someone else. Can you think of one visible, proud, commonality between you and thousands of professionals in the job market? Maybe even at your dream company or industry? If you were going to say "alumni network", we wouldn't give you any brownie points since it's spelled out for you in the chapter heading, but at least we know you're with us!

The alumni network is a bond that is shared by all alumni from your university. In most cases you've shared the same "home" for a period of time, similar experiences around your campus, and maybe even the same major or activities which instantly give you something to talk about. Think about it. Do you have any paraphernalia from your school like a t-shirt or hat? Why did you buy these? Because you're damn proud of where you went to school, and you want to share that with the public. Well, having been out of school over two years now, we can all agree that we're equally proud of our universities and are more than willing to give a leg up to fellow alumni and students who we assume are of the same caliber as we are.

Now just because you have something in common doesn't give you free reign to do and say what you want and still expect that person you're speaking with to help you. Execution is key, which is why we spoke with an expert in leveraging the alumni network: Tim Devane. An alumnus of Wesleyan University, Tim graduated in 2009 during arguably the worst job market in history. While you may say there have been improvements in the market as of early 2013, promising jobs for new graduates are still difficult to find and hyper-competitive to land given the laws of supply and demand.

And while we'll get to the alumni strategy in due time, we want to set the stage about what hard work can honestly mean. As an English major, Tim didn't have a specific track for which he was being groomed. He knew that entrepreneurship and early stage finance interested him, but he really didn't know what that meant and how he could make a career out of it given his major. After bouncing around Washington, D.C. post graduation, he got fed up knowing that he wasn't on the right career path. So he sold his car and moved to the Big Apple on a whim. Without any leads on a job, and only the money from selling his car in his pocket, Tim decided he was going to create a career for himself somehow, someway.

Living on friends' couches and turning his job search into a full-time effort, he risked everything to be in the city that never sleeps. And whether it was the springs in the couch, or the cold, hard reality of post-graduate life, Tim spent all his time contacting different alumni who might understand his pain and be able to help him out. Tim classified his leads into two groups of alumni to better focus his efforts:

1. **Within 5 Years:** These are the alumni who can most likely relate to your frustration and the overall process you're going through. All young professionals at this point in time have seen the impact from the job market, directly or indirectly. Maybe you shared a drink at a party with this person, or you had that one useless elective together that neither of you cared about but managed to pass the time. No matter what, these are the people you can reach out to via text or a Facebook message and say, "Hey, what are you up to? How about we grab a quick coffee?" These are the people who will always give you the time of day. They may not be able to hire you directly, or make the biggest splash with their internal recommendation, but you can bank on them sharing their experience and referring you to anyone they may know within their network.

Finding relevant contacts: easy
Getting in contact: easy
Return on time invested: low/medium

2. **Established Professionals:** Despite having grown up in a different generation, and though they may prefer different formalities and means of getting in contact, at the end of the day you're both alumni with a common interest. This group of alumni can be found within your university's alumni or career database but will require effort and relentless follow-through on your part. If you show passion and a genuine desire to speak with them, when you do connect they can be your Sacajawea—offering key insight and guidance, even using their seniority to get you to where you want to be a lot quicker than you could do on your own.

Finding relevant contacts: medium
Getting in contact: medium/hard
Return on time investment: medium/high

Tim learned quickly this was an incredibly involved process. It required relentless follow up with every solicited person, and a wake up call to check his ego at the door because he faced a lot of rejection despite the sheer volume of communications (email, phone, text, etc.) he made.

It's all too easy to contact the alumni you know, or send out one email per person and leave it at that if you don't hear anything. More often than not you'll find your friends complaining that they're doing everything and striking out. News flash, this does work! It just takes time and resilience to push through. You just may meet the *right* alumni who can open up doors you never thought existed, and you may sift through others who will tell you nothing you didn't already know. But if you stick with this process long enough, it will work out.

So here Tim was, living on 8 inches of foam and springs, hustling day in and day out trying to get time with anyone who would give him a few seconds. He began his outreach to the 5-year range of graduates, all of whom had a few years of experience in an organization under their belts.

Emails led to follow up emails, which eventually led to a response, and finally Tim found himself face-to-face for coffee with these people. The traction eventually started building on itself. Tim offered a ton of insight into the communication process during our interview. One thing he said was, "People generally want to help other people, and as long as you are a good person trying to do good things, everyone will try to help you."

All of this hard work and persistence led Tim to getting in touch with incredibly well-known venture capitalists, who were willing to make the most important intro of Tim's life. As a result of working his alumni network, Tim was introduced to someone at Bit.ly, the company we discussed in Chapter 4 that allows you to track how many clicks there are on a given link. Tim landed a spot as the tenth employee at this start-up.

Now for you good people reading this, we suggest that you check with your school and see if they have an online database for their alumni. This was Tim's bread and butter and his preferred method of finding contact information. If your school has this, you've hit the jackpot. You can in most cases search by profession, age, geographic location, and so much more. We strongly recommend using this tool to build a network of contacts, which you can reach out to when it makes sense. One thing we recommend is using an Excel spreadsheet to keep track of everyone—including their contact information and your current status of that relationship.

Alumni Networking Email Breakdown

With your contacts in place, the key is to write a short, yet effective communication to kick things off. Here is an example letter for you to work with:

Hi David,

I'm a student at the University of Pittsburgh and found your contact information on the alumni database. My background is in Finance and I'm looking to learn more about your career working in Finance at PNC Bank. Would you be willing to spend 20 minutes on the phone with me for an initial discussion?

Thanks in advance for your consideration, and I look forward to hearing from you.

Regards,
Matt

Easy enough, right? Short, sweet, and shows that you're look-ing for a harmless conversation. As a fellow alumnus, your suc-cess rate should be very high. Just be sure to customize the message to cater to your audience.

While there is a method to executing this strategy effectively, which we've just detailed, there is one final point that needs to be stressed. Rushing this process will not give you the results you want. During your job search, there will be times where you get tired and want the quick fix. Let us be very clear: In most cases, using the alumni network is not a quick fix, but it could be the right fix to get you working where you want to be. Going into the first meeting or two saying, "I need a job, can you give me one?" will close the door on that relation-ship quicker than a sorority girl getting drunk at orientation. Remember, be genuine, show true interest in their story, share your background, and take this as an opportunity to build a relationship. Ask lots of questions, and use this person as a sounding board or resource throughout your process. And who knows, they may even help you get the very job you want. The goal here is to build the relationship and then ask for help, not the other way around. On that note, if there are any University of Pittsburgh or Carnegie Mellon students reading this, feel free to get in touch!

CHAPTER SEVENTEEN

TAKING A RABBIT TO TASK
SPENCER BRYAN

D o you remember wanting something? Wanting it so bad that you'd be willing to do just about anything to have it? You'd think about whatever you wanted over and over and over again, to the point where you convinced yourself that if you focused your mind on it long enough, then sure enough it would have to happen.

It's no secret that getting a job in today's climate is very difficult, and it isn't out of the ordinary that we experience that desperate desire to work at a particular company. Whether it's Google or Goldman Sachs or [insert your dream company here], you have probably at some point convinced yourself that this company is the absolute only place you can see yourself working. Does this sound familiar? Maybe it's not one, but rather a handful of companies. Either way, there is a shortlist of places that you dream about, and you're willing to do whatever it takes to get there.

Rather than doing anything and everything, it's very important to find what you want, and focus your energy on getting there.

To help us share this technique, we spoke with Spencer Bryan, an Ole Miss alum and current MBA student at Dartmouth. Spencer had quite a unique experience landing a job at Task-Rabbit upon graduating from Ole Miss. In case you haven't heard of or used TaskRabbit before, it's an application that allows you to hire people for different tasks. So with Spencer's parents visiting him in town, he wanted a table at his favorite restaurant, which didn't take reservations. Instead of asking his parents to wait with him in line during the middle of winter, he hired someone on TaskRabbit to wait for him. Thirty minutes later, Spencer was enjoying his favorite pasta meal (paid for by his parents, of course) without delay, and all it cost him was a few bucks to hire someone to stand in line. He was sold on the idea of TaskRabbit and thought that the startup could have legs to grow. Spencer knew he wanted to be a part of the team that helped to make TaskRabbit big.

Determined to land a job there, he wanted a way to get noticed by the people who could hire him. It's here that we'll pause, and ask you whether or not you've heard of judo. Maybe you've taken lessons in this form of martial arts or have been on the receiving end of someone else's judo skills. Hopefully not, but the most fundamental element of judo is to use your opponent's strength to your advantage. Sounds simple enough, right?

It starts with identifying the company/companies for which you'd like to work, and writing down the things they do well. For instance, using the TaskRabbit example, they bring together the people looking to have something done with the people willing to do that task. Since Spencer was trying to land a job, he wanted to speak with someone about interviewing at Task-Rabbit. So once he posted that request, it was a no-brainer for someone at TaskRabbit to respond. Boom. Spencer was in. It's safe to say in the early days of this company that no one else was doing this, which earned him huge points for originality. After a good chat with his new contact at TaskRabbit, an offer shortly followed.

Now we should also mention that Spencer did his homework on the company. He knew their goals and challenges, and he had thought about why he wanted to work there over anywhere else, so once in the interview, he came across as someone who could genuinely add value to TaskRabbit.

Thinking about how you could apply this to whichever company you want to work for, don't forget to keep it simple. The goal here is to find out what the company does, replicate that in your own way, and get it in front of someone at the company for feedback. It just so happened that the TaskRabbit example catered to speaking directly with someone, but in most cases that won't happen. Be creative, and show that you can think outside of the box.

This technique is one that separates the men from the boys, as the saying goes, since you'll need to go above and beyond everyone else who is applying blindly. There are no instructions, other than KISS (keep it simple, stupid). If you want to work on Wall Street, you could use a free investing account (visit investopedia.com or similar site) to trade for 30 days and write up a report showing your performance requesting input on how your strategy matches up with the company's. Maybe you want to work in the fashion industry so you design a piece of clothing to give to someone at your target firm and request some feedback on the style from the company's perspective.

Maybe you want to work in a role that isn't directly related to the company's product, like the supply chain for a clothing company. You could do an industry analysis on the raw materials the company purchases and sell your research, according to your understanding of the company's challenges (and of course throw in some ideas for combating those challenges). That's a pretty compelling story in front of someone at your target company. You'll almost guarantee yourself an "in" when you bring something to the table before asking for something.

As always, we're very interested to hear about your success with this technique, so please reach out via www.boldjobbook. com so that we can share your story with others!

CHAPTER EIGHTEEN

HOW TO TAKE THE CHILL OUT OF COLD CALLING
MEGAN TOWE

Networking isn't a linear process where A+B always gives you C. It comes in many different forms and changes over time, especially from one relationship or group to the next. Sometimes it can be very easy where it's nothing more than mingling at a dinner party where you're handing out your card to people that spark your interest. And other times it can be difficult, like when you're trying to get on the phone or have coffee with a specific person who probably doesn't have the time of day for you. Getting in touch with the latter group of people is almost like an art form.

While she has never been a formal artist, we met Megan Towe, who perfected this approach early on. Megan was just a 20-something young professional from Colby College who really wasn't happy with the corporate gig she had landed out of college. Though not entirely sure of her next move, after reading an article while searching current business development opportunities, she knew who she wanted to get in touch with.

His name was Charlie O'Donnell and he was the founder of Brooklyn Bridge Ventures, which made him a gatekeeper in the world of venture capital and all of the companies his fund invested in. An important person in the business world, the sheer volume of cold emails Charlie gets on a daily basis is more than many of us could ever imagine, which is why requests from someone random rarely see daylight.

In February 2011, Megan reached out to Charlie with what may have seemed like a simple cold email to the common eye, but was actually a perfectly crafted message that got Charlie's attention.

"I recently came across your article **"Building a Great Company Culture is Critical When You're a Startup"** ....I found your article during my current search for business development and operations opportunities at young, non-corporate organizations...The article strongly resonated with me and I would love any guidance you may have on pursuing entry-level positions in the startup field."

Charlie gets a lot of these notes, but it just so happened that he was free for breakfast that Monday, so he agreed to meet. That's one aspect that can't be overlooked: timing. The other thing that was important was that she had taken the time to mention not only his article, but also portfolio companies that Brooklyn Bridge Ventures were involved in and why she thought they were interesting. "If you're going to meet with me, it's not hard to figure out which companies we're involved with or that

114

I've worked on specifically," mentioned Charlie in his personal blog post (http://www.thisisgoingtobebig.com/blog/2011/4/1/how-to-get-an-exciting-job-at-an-awesome-startup-in-less-tha.html, April 1, 2011) about his interaction with Megan.

That following Monday, Megan met up with Charlie for a quick breakfast. She knew she had to make the most of her time with Charlie so she made sure to key in on any hints or important names he dropped during their meeting. Megan knew Charlie was her *in* to an endless amount of opportunities in the startup world, but she had to prove herself to him before he would have the confidence to back her.

As soon as their breakfast was over, Megan found the contact information for a name Charlie mentioned in their meeting who played a big role in the biz dev community, Alex Taub. She sent Alex a cold email using Charlie as a reference and just offered her time and talent to help him in any way possible.

Less than two hours after their breakfast, Charlie received the first of two things that won him over.

The first was an email from Alex, who he never formally introduced to Megan, saying:

"Megan reached out and I'm sitting down with her. She can help with organizing the event."

The second thing showed up at his office the next morning:

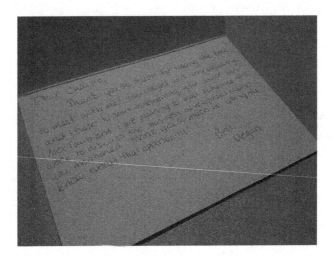

The impression Megan made on Charlie landed her a big win only one week later. LiveIntent, a company in Charlie's portfolio was looking for an "inexperienced hard charging media sales account manager". One can only guess who was top of mind for Charlie's recommendation.

Charlie talks about the five key components to successfully networking in his blog, and we definitely recommend you read the full post here. But to save you time, we'll sum up our three favorites. The first and most important step is that you have to **reach out**. As we all know, if you don't try, you will fail 100% of the time. Another important factor is that you must **be different**. Important people get millions of cold emails, why should your target contact read yours? Lastly, **offer value**. An important aspect that helped Megan win was that she offered value when she reached out to Alex.

So what are you waiting for? Get to writing those emails to the people you want to meet! Use the guide below to ensure your email makes it to the top of the inbox.

Email Subject Line Breakdown

Another important thing to remember when reaching out to someone with a cold email is the art of a subject line. As someone who has had to learn to do this the right way in her email pursuits, we've worked with Megan in order to break down this process and make it ridiculously easy for you to become a master of the subject line.

Taking a step back and looking at the email itself, it doesn't matter what you write inside if it doesn't get read. You could have a killer opener, the funniest punch line, even a singing cat that would make anyone howl with laughter. But if you don't write a killer subject line, your email will *never be opened*, especially with a cold email. Take some advice from MailChimp, the company that sends thousands of marketing emails a day:

> "When it comes to email marketing, the best subject lines tell what's inside, and the worst subject lines sell what's inside."

To do this, follow these simple rules which are inspired by MailChimp:

Do:
- Set your subscribers' expectations and clearly state what's inside the email
- **Use words such as:** Apply, opportunity, demo, connect, payments, conference, cancellation
- If targeting a company, mention something about an article they've been in (ex. Congrats on your funding!)
- Send before 6am
- Use a name the person is familiar with in the subject line
- Subject lines that have worked:
  - "Had lunch with Alexander Ljung"—that works. Alex is the founder of our portfolio company Soundcloud
  - "Twitter board date change"—that double works. Portfolio company name and very descriptive.
  - "ECB violation"—sadly that works. But please don't send me emails with that subject line.

Don't:
- Write your subject lines like advertisements
- Write a generic subject line
- Look like a scam
  - Go into your junk mail and take a look at what *not* to write
- **Words not to use:** Confirm, join, assistance, speaker, press, social, invite

- Subject lines that didn't work:
  - "Two things"—that doesn't work. Two things is worse than one thing, and isn't descriptive.
  - "Pleasure speaking with you"—that doesn't work. I speak to so many people every day. Not nearly descriptive enough.
  - "I know you are a busy man"—that doesn't work. Not descriptive.

Always remember that you're not trying to trick anyone during your job search. You've done the hard work already earning your degree and gaining the experience that qualifies you. There is an abundance of other equally qualified people applying for the same job as you, which naturally reduces your chances of standing out. Don't let that happen. Take control by communicating directly, and be sure to use subject lines that get you read, not trashed.

To measure the effectiveness of your emails, one thing you can do within Gmail is request a read receipt to see if you're email has gotten through. This is not 100% accurate, but it's accurate enough to get a really good idea of whether you're being seen or not.

If you request a read receipt, requests will be sent to every recipient in the **To:** and **Cc:** fields.

1. Compose a message as usual while using the desktop version of Gmail at mail.google.com.
2. Click the **More options** icon in the compose window.

3. Click **Request read receipt.**
4. Send your message.

This is just one quick and easy tip with big results for giving you the information you need during your campaign.

CHAPTER NINETEEN

DEVELOPING SUSTAINABLE RELATIONSHIPS
NICK GAVRONSKY

Let's get back to something we've discussed already. Whether you consciously think about it or not, you represent a brand. This brand is visible in everything you do. So stop for a second and think of what that brand is.

- How does it look?
- What message does it sell?
- Would you want to buy "your brand"?

This brand represents you, your own agent standing in front of a company ready to make a job offer. All of the creative techniques and methods in the world can't change the fact that when it comes time for a decision to be made, the applicant will be assessed by the image they portray, the passion they show, and their track record of doing something positive.

The market calls this acquisition of human talent/capital "hiring," but in reality, it's an investment. Company X is making an investment in a person, and they expect a return of some kind above and beyond that investment. And what easier way to quickly seal the deal than by having your brand give your target company the confidence to invest in you.

To put this into context, we had a great chat with the Head of Product for OpenFin, Nick Gavronsky. A graduate of the University of Miami where he studied Finance, Nick's story starts when he entered the workforce as an analyst in Citi Group's rotational program back in 2008. Gaining exposure across a number of different banking disciplines, one of his final rotations involved mobile banking, which led to a more permanent role in NYC focusing specifically on this category.

Despite being content at Citi Group, Nick's desire to work for a startup began to increase as time passed. He attended various MeetUp groups (see: www.meetup.com), developed a blog, and actively participated in different networking groups within the city. Once Nick's day job ended, he was busy working on himself and doing something above and beyond the average nine-to-fiver.

As fate would have it, at one of these MeetUp events focused on FinTech (or finance technology) Nick met two previously successful entrepreneurs who had just launched a new company: OpenFin. Truly in awe, Nick thought he might like to work with them in the future.

Fast-forward nearly two months. Nick continued to run into the founders of OpenFin at various events and industry forums. While most events are structured around a specific topic or industry, he increasingly got the sense that their conversations would drift from casual industry chit-chat to more pointed questions, almost like a job interview.

Meanwhile, throughout all of this he continued to keep his blog running, alongside a demanding day job, and continuously networked, i.e. built his brand. After months of chatting and several serious discussions (as a result of the increasingly pointed questions), sure enough an offer to join OpenFin materialized. The offer wasn't only on the basis that the two entrepreneurs thought Nick had the right skills and experience to be working for them, but that he was a genuine person with a true passion for mobile finance. This came through loud and clear in his consistent commitment in the industry to be "out there" in the community.

When summarizing this story, Nick didn't forget to mention to us that he had honestly never applied for a job at OpenFin. Like Scott discussed (see Chapter 15), Nick focused on doing the right things over and over again, and the people around him took notice.

Now for the twenty-dollar (or whatever you paid for this book) question of the hour, how does this apply to you?

For starters, let's break down the 3 things we recommend doing from here on out:

1. Join a local industry group
   a. Use sites like MeetUp.com or search for your industry (e.g. Finance Group Philadelphia) on Google.

      Tip: being nervous or unsure of yourself when attending these types of events is completely normal, especially if you're younger. Remember, you have instant friends and connections waiting for you since you have similar interests as everyone else there.

2. Join an industry group on LinkedIn
   a. Look for local discussion threads to which you can contribute one post or comment each week. Any opportunity to take a conversation off the group and in person with another user is a big win for several reasons. First, you'll increase your industry presence online by adding that person as a connection. Second, you'll have a connection to reach out to should you ever want to work at their company or sync up with one of their connections directly. Odds are, if you engage a person that works in the same city that you go to school or work in, your paths will end up crossing which makes attending the events listed in the first point above even easier.

3. Take an internship: paid or unpaid
   a. Taking an unpaid internship or moonlighting can help you obtain the skills and experiences you need to be taken seriously with your target employer. In Chapter 15, we talk about what Scott Britton (Top 25 under 25 NYC, CEO of Sfter.com, BD @ SinglePlatform) did to make the jump using this strategy.

This technique likely isn't one where you'll see immediate results. However, doing this right over a period of time will help you build your network and put you in a very powerful position when it comes time to getting a job or exploring new opportunities. And honestly, if done right you will never need to seek out another job opportunity as they will now come to you. It's sustainable, and most importantly, it's fun because you get to connect with other people that share your interests.

CHAPTER TWENTY

JUST A CONVERSATION
BETWEEN FRIENDS
JUSTIN MARES

Let's take a second to think about what the actual process to landing a job involves. On a high level, we've broken this down into the following steps:

- Company X has a need, and requires talent to deliver on that need
- Company X determines what skills and experience level are needed within that talent
- Potential applicants determine if their own skills and experiences are enough of a fit to apply
- Company X selects a small pool of applicants that match their minimum requirements on paper
- Company X conducts one or several rounds of vetting to determine personality and fit, character, and in many cases the true ability behind the skills and experiences listed within the resume
- The applicant with the greatest number of matches against Company X's requirements will ultimately get the job offer

There is a lot happening here in a very short amount of time. It can be intense, especially for the more competitive positions. But wouldn't it be nice if you could more or less be in control of your own personal assessment AND build strong connections as a byproduct?

Justin Mares think so, and we have to agree with him.

As former CEO of Roommate Fit and current Director of Revenue at Exceptional Cloud Service, Justin boasts having never applied to a single job, at least not in the traditional sense as described above.

The key to getting in this position is by building a deep and strong network of people in your target industry or company that understand who you are and what you can do in advance of that day when you are need of a job. From a strategy perspective, building a network like this takes time, energy, and focus, but it will deliver sustainable, long-term results into the future.

What Justin has made a living on is helping others. Offering up his energy to those who either have a recognized need but don't have the time or resources to address it, or by identifying needs that may not even be apparent to that particular person.

Focusing on influential people in your industry, or the industry you want to get involved with, it's remarkably easy to identify what most people are working on. Heck, LinkedIn will tell you all that and then some.

Using Justin as an example, he had just taken a course on Mixergy.com and noticed a lot of opportunity to improve how the company was engaging with its users. Recognizing this as an opportunity to sync up with Andrew Warner (formerly the co-founder and CEO of Bradford & Reed (top 25 website in early 2000s) and current CEO of entrepreneurial education site Mixergy.com), he simply dropped him an email. Short and sweet, Justin pointed out an opportunity for his company to improve the course and gain more customers. Free help, and a plan to deliver results: what could be better? Not surprisingly, Andrew gladly connected with Justin on the phone for several calls and eventually reaped the benefits.

At this point, Justin had proved he had skill, strong communication, and credibility behind his words. The relationship was formed with mutual respect, and now Justin was personally connected with one of the big shots in his target industry, tech.

It wasn't long after establishing this valuable connection with Andrew Warner that Justin began writing a book addressing a topic in the tech industry. As part of the research and development phase, he needed advice and support from someone influential in tech. Boom—he didn't have to look farther than his connection with Andrew to get what he needed. He had a figurehead from the industry as a personal connection who agreed to support him, returning the favor.

Friends help friends out, plain and simple. You just need to make sure you have the right ones in the proper industry. Start helping others by reaching out to demonstrate your value. Offer up something that helps them and become friends with these connections. As the relationship develops, opportunities may arise; a job opening at that company and they think of you, for example. Or maybe like Justin you're in need of advice or support, and your connections can open the door. Once the relationship is in place, and you've demonstrated your value, the process described at the beginning of this chapter is fast-tracked and simplified down to a conversation between friends. This takes serious time and effort, but it is essential to improving your position and security within your industry.

YOU'VE GOT MAIL AND MAIL AND MAIL
SCOTT BRITTON

Having the stickiest subject line is great, but it only works if you have your targets email address, and kick-ass cold-email body to support. In Chapter 15, we talked about fighting for your place in the job market and used the examples from Scott Britton to provide context. As it turns out Scott is something of a cold-email guru as a result of his current role running Business Development for SinglePlatform. In an effort to give you the best, Scott has provided us with his guides to finding any email for any person, and the structure to writing them an email that is bound to get a response.

Originally published on his blog, Life-Longlearner.com, these two posts have been reformatted and edited for this book:

How to Find Anyone's Email Addresses

Business development for me usually means knocking on doors. In the digital world, that door is your inbox. Sometimes targets make my life easy by listing their email on their site. But just like the YellowPages, many people prefer to be "unlisted" online. This requires me to be resourceful to find email addresses.

After I have identified the name of the person I need to reach, here is how I find their email address:

Rapportive trick

The first stop for me is the <u>Rapportive</u> trick. When I enter the correct email in Gmail, Rapportive will often populate my target's other digital profiles. To guess the correct email I start by plugging in popular email syntaxes followed by the company's domain name:

> first initial +last name@companyname.com
> last name@companyname.com
> first name@companyname.com
> first name+last name@companyname.com
> first initial+last initial@companyname.com
> first initial+last name@companyname.com
> first initial.lastname@companyname.com
> first initial@companyname.com

If Rapportive populates a profile, I know I have guessed correctly. Note the difference:

Incorrect Email

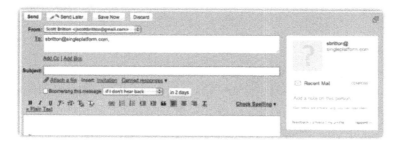

Correct Email

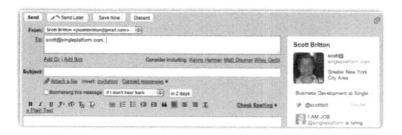

There are frequent instances where you may have guessed correctly, yet Rapportive does not populate a profile. This occurs because their data sources (Rapleaf amongst others) does not possess additional information for that email.

I start this process with Rapportive because in addition to determining the target's email address, it also gives me additional context such as tweets and links to their various digital presences. These all provide potential touchpoints for a connection which makes cold outreach more effective. "Hey noticed on

Twitter you're an Eagles fan. I was super bummed about the loss too. Anyways..."

MailTester

If Rapportive fails, I move to MailTester.com. This service checks whether email addresses are attached to a specific domain then determines whether the name combination you're trying is correct. This is valuable because it first determines whether you're guessing the right domain. Often large companies have separate domains for email than the one their native website resides on. MailTester enables me to determine whether this is the case. Once I have the domain correct, I begin to plug in the popular syntaxes highlighted above. If the server allows email address verification, MailTester will let me know if I've guessed correctly.

Incorrect

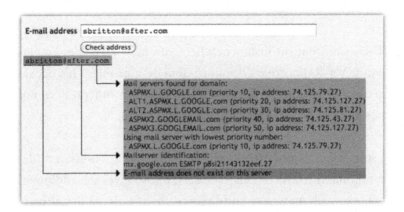

Correct

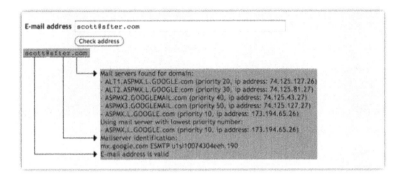

Again, sometimes this doesn't work with Mail Tester because they do not permit email address verification. That looks like this:

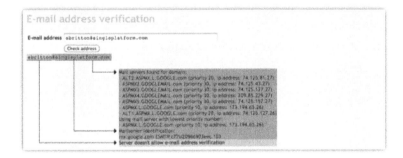

Jigsaw/Data.com

When Rapportive and MailTester don't work, I hit up Jigsaw/Data.com. It's a contributory contact database that is free to join. After you've exhausted you're credit for free contacts, you can exchange your Rolodex for access to target emails.

If they have the contact I'm looking for I double check the email address provided via Rapportive and MailTester. Because all the content is user-generated there is some poor information here, so it gives me peace of mind to double check.

If they don't have the specific contact I'm looking for, I'll obtain the contact information for two different people at that company to try in order to determine the syntax. When I do this, I try to get the most recently added contacts and make sure they were added on different dates. Why? Because I want fresh data and people often batch phony information.

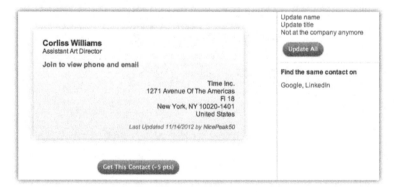

Google Your Best Guess

If you have still not been able to find the person's email address your looking for there is still hope. Often people put their email on pdf's such as press releases which appear in search results. So go ahead and Google the popular syntax combinations.

Call and Ask

Find the main phone number on the website and call the organization you're trying to reach. Tell the receptionist you were trying to send something important to x and politely ask if you could have this person's email address.

I know talking to an actual person might be scary, but relax. You're not asking the receptionist out on a date. You're asking her for information. It's her job to provide this to you. She won't tell you to bow your head in shame after this request. I promise. Pick up the phone.

Go Rogue. Hit their Personal Email

When all hope seems lost, I do something I don't like doing. I try the Rapportive trick with my best guess of their personal Gmail. When a profile populates I cross check with whatever social profile appears to verify that this is the person I'm trying to reach. Although it can feel like you're crossing over sacred ground, if your offering is truly a value add and you're able to convey this effectively, people will appreciate you reaching out.

I always preface these emails with:

"Hey x,

Apologies for pinging you on your personal email here, but I couldn't find any other way of contacting you"

If you're hesitant to do this, think about what you have to gain vs. lose. I never hit a shot I didn't take.

Register.com

If you're dealing with a small site (1-2 person operation), you may still be stranded on the unlisted island even after doing all of these things. At this point, I'll go to register.com and do a reverse who is lookup for whatever domain owner I'm trying to reach. If the domain is not private which is often the case, I'll be provided with the owner's contact email. Believe it or not, I've gotten a deal through this.

Emails for Corporations

Emails for corporations is a free resource that provides the business email address patterns for over 1000 companies. It also provides other valuable information such as the corporate phone number.

One feature that I really like is that I'm able to search by industry and geographical location. These facets are valuable for prospecting.

Company Name	HQ Metro Area	HQ State Abbreviation	Email Convention	Email Domain	Example (Jane Francis Doe)	Notes	Main Phone Number
Sort ↓	Sort ↓	Sort ↓	Sort ↓	Sort ↓	Sort ↓	Sort ↓	Sort ↓
Boeing Corporation	Chicago	IL	First.MiddleInitial.La st	boeing.com	Jane.F.Doe@boein g.com		312-544-2000
CACI, Inc.	Washington	DC	FirstInitialLastName	caci.com	JDoe@caci.com		703-841-7800
Computer Sciences Corporation (sub of Convansys)	Falls Church	VA	FirstInitialLastName	csc.com	JDoe@csc.com		703.876.1000
Goodrich Corporation	Charlotte	NC	Firstname.Lastnam e	goodrich.com	Jane.Doe@goodric h.com		704.423.7000

Toofr

Toofr is another email database that I've called upon to find email addresses. It claims to have email addresses for over 400k companies. I've used it a few times and I'd say 80% of the time its correct. They start you out with 10 free attempts, but after that you need to pay. Considering, there's a bunch of free alternatives I only go here as a last resort.

CEO Email Addresses

CEO Email addresses is exactly what it sounds like. Not surprisingly sometimes the CEO'S email address doesn't match the syntax of the rest of the company. Other times it does. Either way this is a valuable resource to find email addresses for the folks hanging in the c-suite.If you use these methodologies there is about a 95% chance you can find about any target's email address. Otherwise there is always the contact form.

Now go knock on some doors!

How to Ask for An Email Introduction

There are effective practices when asking for email introduction that respect the time and circumstance of all parties. I've really come to appreciate these and wish more people approached introduction requests this way.

Here's how I approach asking for an email introduction:

Step 1: Preliminary Request for An Introduction

You've identified that someone in your network is connected to the person you're trying to reach. Send them a brief preliminary intro request to gauge the strength of their relationship and willingness to connect. An example script:

Hi X,

I was looking to get introduced to Johnny Dealmaker from Project X and saw you were connected to him. Not sure how well you're connected to him, but if the relationship is strong, I'd really appreciate an intro to chat about ways to work with my Project Y. Please let me know if you feel comfortable doing this and I'll forward over a proper request for introduction that you can forward to him.

Thanks!
Scott

Key elements of this email:

1. **The Ask**—*"I was looking to get introduced to Johnny Dealmaker from Project X and saw you were connected to him"* If you're asking for an introduction, skip the dog and pony show and ask for it in the first 2 sentences. A clear understanding of how someone can help is always appreciated.

2. **Consideration of the Connecting Parties Relationship**— *"If the relationship is strong; Please let me know if you feel comfortable doing this"* As the person being asked for an intro, I never like to make introductions when I don't know if both parties will benefit.

There are people that I've met for 48 seconds at a networking event who connected with me on LinkedIn. When someone asks to be introduced to these people, I lack the context to assess how mutually beneficial an introduction will be. As a result, I don't feel comfortable making introductions to them.

Alternatively, maybe I do know them well, but I just had an awkward interaction with them. The last thing I feel like doing is emailing them for an intro request.

The bottom line is I appreciate when someone acknowledges that not all connections are people I feel comfortable making an introduction to. Framing the request with this in mind makes the ask a whole lot more manageable and is just a courteous practice.

3. **The Why**—*"I'd really appreciate an intro to chat about ways to work with Project Y"*
The why gives me the ability to determine whether both parties will benefit. Everyone has demands on their time, so it's important as a brokering party to make sure you're adding value when connecting someone.

4. **Make It Easy for the Connecting Party**—*"I'll forward over a proper request for introduction that you can forward to him."*
The connecting party is doing you a favor by making an introduction. The least you can do is make it as easy as

possible for them to do this. Making them formulate in their own words why they're connecting you guys requires effort. Sending something that they can forward along with appropriate context limits the work.

Step 2: Proper Request For An Introduction

After you've got confirmation that the connecting party feels comfortable making an introduction, it's time for the proper request for an introduction. This email contains similar elements to the first one, but with some additional context because it will be forwarded to your target. An example script:

Hey X,

Was hoping that you might be able to introduce me to Johnny Dealmaker at Project X.

I wanted to connect with him because our email list targets a similar demographic with limited overlap. Seeing as our products are non-competitive, I wanted to touch base to see if he was up for brainstorming ways to leverage our existing user bases to grow both of our lists.

We did this with Company R in the past, and both parties received a 15% lift in new subscribers.

Any help is much appreciated.
Scott

Key Elements:

1. **Explicit Ask**—This indicates to the target that someone approached them about connecting.
2. **Compelling Context Why**—Here you should expand upon why this person should spend time connecting with you. This serves to legitimize the ask from the connecting party and provides context for the target to assess whether connecting is worthwhile. Your goal is to put your best foot forward in a concise manner.
3. **Strengthening Example**—I think it's always effective to mention a past success or current partner. It provides credibility. In an era of cyborg spam filters, this is very important even when an introduction brokers an interaction.
4. **Appreciation**—Again this person is doing you a favor.

At this point, the hope is that the target indicates they're interested in connecting and your mutual connection proceeds to make the introduction.

I like this methodology because it respects the time and circumstances of all parties. Because you've given each party the option to opt in, obligatory feelings are limited (to the extent they can be). This makes for a better conversation with the target and relationship with the person you're asking an introduction from.

To find out more about Scott, you can visit his blog (www. life-longlearner.com), or follow him on twitter (@britton).

DREAMING BIG

CHAPTER TWENTY-ONE

THEY SEE SOMETHING IN ME
NEIL EVERETT

This next story is a bit more personal than the others we have shared so far. Our very own Melanie, co-author of this book, has agreed to share her incredible story that allowed her to meet her favorite sportscaster at ESPN. Here's Mel's story in her own words!

Desperate to find a job after graduating from college, I was watching a webinar on networking. At the end I was given an assignment: Reach out to someone that you think you have no chance of getting in touch with. My dream job after college was always to work for ESPN, so I figured I would give it a try by emailing my favorite sportscaster, Neil Everett. He had no publicly listed information of course, so I had a to get a little creative. I was connected with a few people on LinkedIn who worked for ESPN, so I took the pattern of their email address and put together three or four possible email addresses that could be Neil's and sent off a heartfelt email. I gave it a shot, but I set no expectations.

One month later, I had a missed call and voicemail. It started with, "Hi Mel, this is Neil Everett's voice calling you."

Here's the thing. I saw myself as a nobody, yet here I was on the phone with one of the best sportscasters at ESPN, discussing my interests in working for the company. From that moment, I felt like I had a Superman cape on and could do anything. I applied this courage and effort to my job search. After that call, I had interview after interview, and two weeks later I flew from my hometown in Hawaii to New York City, where I started my new job and adventure, which was not at ESPN, but another job I was equally excited about.

Fast-forward to ten months later. I was sitting in a coffee shop grinding away on this very eBook, the book that was drawn from the inspiration of a single voicemail. During a break from my book, I came across a YouTube video that caught my interest. It was of Neil Everett, speaking at a University Club, telling his story about how he landed his job at ESPN. It was amazing and inspiring, and I was determined to interview him for my book.

Excitedly, I immediately emailed Neil, but of course it was not going to be that easy. After about ten emails, and finally a phone call that started off as, "How do I know you again?", I was able to tell him about my book and how he was an inspiration in writing it. He agreed to do an interview, but he didn't do Skype or any sort of video interviews so it would have to be over the phone. While I was happy just to have his time, I wanted a video interview so badly. I knew I wasn't going to get his full in-depth story over a phone call where I would be desperately trying to write everything down as he was talking.

So I took a gamble. "What if I was in LA this weekend, could we do this in person? We wouldn't have to do a video interview, as I know you are a private person, but could I record your voice so I can at least document everything?" His response felt better than Christmas morning. "Melanie, if you are in LA this weekend, we can do a video interview, in person, and I will give you a tour of my studio." And so two days later, I was on a plane to LA from NYC.

You may think, "Why would an ESPN sportscaster's story be relevant to someone who just graduated from college and is struggling to land their first job?" I will admit, I was a little nervous his story would be too far removed from my audience, but I was very happily proven wrong.

Neil's story starts like this, and is so much better told in his voice: "My first job ever in Hawaii, just to show you that there is hope, was holding a sign at the corner of Punchbowl and Baretania that said 'Shoes By Michael: Going Out of Business'. The light would be green, I would hold it this way, and then the light would turn green here I would hold it this way. I did that for eight hours in my early twenties for the whole summer. So don't give up, you can work your way up from the bottom to the top."

Along with holding a sign for eight hours a day, Neil worked part time at Sizzler and failed at getting a job as a Polynesian dancer (though he's still not sure why). After that summer, Neil went back to finish up his last two years of school at the University of Oregon where he earned his journalism degree. Hawaii was always in the back of his mind because he felt it was such a special place and knew he wanted to live there long-term. After one year of working on the Oregon coast, he moved to Maui and worked as a board operator at a radio station. Three months into that job, Hawaii Pacific College was advertising for a Sports Information Director position, and he was able to land that position based on his experience.

For the next fifteen years, Neil worked at Hawaii Pacific University mostly in sports information and athletic administration. On the side, he was able to get in with local television.

"One job-securing lesson would be, finesse. That is what I used to get into local television. There were just three television stations at the time, and I had sent them each my resume before I had moved to Hawaii along with a little reel of what I had done as an intern, which is just about as sketch[y] as you can get, but it's something. I sent it to them. I followed up. They tell you to follow up in a month, you mark that down in your calendar and one month later you call them back. That is finesse as opposed to being a pain in the *okole* (Hawaiian for "butt")."

On nights where Neil didn't have games at Hawaii Pacific University, he would go down to KITV, the local news station, where he worked as the production assistant, writing copy for the 10 o'clock news. One weekend they realized all their sports guys were going to be gone, and Neil was given his first big break to be the sportscaster for the news station that week.

Eventually Neil transitioned into sports director at Channel 9 News and worked at Hawaii Pacific part time. At the time, Neil really could not imagine a better life for himself.

"We had a lot of athletes go through Hawaii Pacific, where I worked closely. One kid specifically was from Rhode Island. His name was Brandon Murphy. He is still a friend of mine to-day; I just talked with him yesterday. He was in New York after he had graduated, and he was working out at a club. He started a conversation with the guy on the treadmill on the machine next to him. This guy was a sports agent and Brandon said, 'You should check out my boy in Hawaii'. The next thing I new this guy had called me up and said, 'I want to represent you'. I told him that he couldn't do anything for me. I live in Hawaii, a big fish in a small pond. I don't know what clicked inside my head in this conversation, and this is what I tell young people out there, this is when you determine what your golden ring is. How high you want to reach and what you want to be. Some-thing clicked in my mind and I said, 'You get me an interview at ESPN, and we will talk.' I had never ever dreamt about work-ing at ESPN. I never considered it, and I never thought my skillset was such that I could make it. It had never crossed my mind, but I knew that was the Mount Rushmore of what I did."

A few months later, Neil received an unexpected call. "I got you the interview at ESPN, get on the next plane to Bristol." Some things, you just cannot explain or even begin to understand, this may be one of them.

Neil flew to Bristol, Connecticut for the interview of a lifetime. "I did not do my homework, and I thought I was going to cool my way through. I bombed it. I was horrible. They basically had us do a miniature sports center, and I couldn't have kicked it any worse."

Neil came back to Hawaii with his tail between his legs. All he wanted to do was represent Hawaii on the biggest stage possible, and he knew he blew it. He failed to prepare. As hard as it was, Neil continued to do his thing. If the worst thing in life was getting rejected from ESPN, he knew his life wasn't so bad.

One year later, Neil got a call back from his agent, who said, "They saw something."

This time Neil prepared. He did his homework. "This time I studied and this time I went back there, and I thought I knocked it out of the park. I was patting myself on the back and I thought, 'Gosh, they are going to hire me before I even walk out of the building.' Apparently I wasn't [that great], because now I come back to

Hawaii and it's another whole full year. Now I can't even watch Sports Center because all I think about is how I blew it again."

Neil never found out the reason why, but eventually he got the call back from his agent a year later, and this time the agent asked Neil if he could be there in two weeks because he got the job. Neil said, "How about two months because we are going to have a going away party that is going to be epic."

To put Neil's wisdom into action, and to lean on David Letterman's "Top 10" for some flavor, here are **Neil Everett's top 10 pieces of advice for recent college grads:**

1. **Do your research on the company for which you want to work**

   "The lesson learned is to know as much as you can and don't think you know too much before you go in for that interview."

2. **Finesse**

   "If they tell you to call them back in a month, you mark it down in your calendar, and one month later you call them back. That's finesse as opposed to being a pain in the *okole*.

3. **Skill, hard work, and luck**

   "I think I had a skillset that I am a good writer. I worked hard, sixty, seventy, eighty hours a week for a lot of years, and I got so lucky it will make me cry to think how lucky I got. I didn't get one call from ESPN; I got two."

4. Get in the building

"The guy who ran ESPN for the longest time, started in the mailroom. The guy who was my boss for the longest time, started in the mailroom. And the point being, you need to get in the room."

5. Treat your internships like gold

"I always say that was the most important college class I ever took, my internship."

6. Perseverance

"A friend of mine shared a story with me. He was a big, heavy guy. He said, 'I am going to ask a hundred girls out for a date, if I get 99 nos, that means I got a date. He wasn't worried about the nos because he was just looking for one yes. The point being is that you have just got to keep firing."

7. Don't make failure an option

"I never thought about it not working. If you don't have a place to land, you walk that tight wire a lot more carefully."

8. Education is your key

"I guess my message would be, college is a great time, but let's keep the order what it should be. One [thing to remember] is your education is your key."

9. Find a mentor

"If I want to be a director at ESPN, then you need to make friends with a director at ESPN or an assistant director and ask them, what are the steps that you would recommend for me to take so that I can someday direct at ESPN?"

10. Don't let rejection determine your self worth

"Just because this person didn't want to hire you, and this person didn't want to hire you, and this person didn't want to hire you, doesn't mean that that next person isn't going to want to hire you, and it doesn't mean that you aren't worthy of being hired."

CHAPTER TWENTY-TWO

DON'T SPAM YOUR FRIENDSHIPS

DAN SHIPPER

D o you remember what it was like when you were 10? When getting a "Fruit by the Foot" rollup in your lunch pretty much made your day? Well whatever it was that got you excited back then, we'd be willing to bet that going head-to-head with Microsoft by building your own competing company wasn't something you thought about much. But for tech guru, FireFly CEO, and current University of Pennsylvania junior Dan Shipper, that's where it all began.

While Microsoft failed to stop and wait for a then-young Dan to get his coding skills up to speed for a real battle, this initial goal and drive has led him on an exciting journey. During this journey, he has started several companies, had a large startup (Y Combinator's 42floors) *publicly* offer him a job (which he declined), and even had another company *publicly* apologize for NOT hiring him when he interviewed for an internship as a freshman in college.

So why are we sharing the story of someone who isn't looking for a job, and in most cases has companies looking for him? It's all because of what he is doing to put himself in this favored position. We had a great chat with him about his methodology, and it's actually quite simple, and is perfect for truly anyone applying for anything. In this case we're focusing on getting a job, but it could also be getting into a school, a club, or anything else that may require an application. It's all about building meaningful relationships with people in the field in which you work or want to break into.

Let's backup to the 42floors story for a second though. 42floors was started by Jason Freedman, an alumnus of Silicon Valley's tech incubation program Y-Combinator. Jason writes an interesting blog that Dan had followed for some time. Liking what he was reading, Dan decided he would share his appreciation with Jason, and before he knew it they were going back and forth.

Sure enough, when 42floors was looking to hire key talent, they took to the Internet to publish their desire to hire Dan:

Dear Dan Shipper:

Please join us. Consider this a job offer to work at 42Floors. Because you have never applied for this position, this may come as a little bit of a surprise. But you have known for a while that I have been really impressed with your work.

You're only a sophomore in college, but you've already started several companies. You've taught yourself to code, and you are a maker at heart. And you have that rare gift of having a sense of style in your design work as well. AND, your blog posts that reach Hacker News are eloquent and well thought out. It would be an honor to have you join us here at 42Floors.

Here is your job description: You will make gorgeous products that help entrepreneurs find their dream office. There are dozens of things we need built -- you will pick what you most want to work on or come up with your own project.

If you ever decide you want to go back to working on your own startup, you have my full support, and I will personally do everything I can to help you be successful as an entrepreneur.

You will never be asked to sign a non-compete. You will be free to contribute to open source, free to blog about anything and everything, and never be required to submit a patent that could be used offensively.

This offer has no expiration and, regardless of whether you decide to work with us, I hope to personally be there on your side in everything you do.

Most sincerely,
Jason Freedman
Co-Founder, 42Floors

Public "I want you!" letters from companies aren't a dime a dozen, especially in the current job climate. Dan had only known Jason for 6 months prior to the publication of the blog post (which went viral, by the way.) Think about your oldest friends. How many of them would go to these lengths to share how valued you are and say that, no matter what, they have your back? This almost never happens. But for anyone who has met Dan, this comes as no surprise simply because he is passionate about what he does and enjoys sharing that passion with those around him. Not to mention, he's incredible at what he does.

Now in our journey to understand and simplify the process for getting a job out of college, the same steps continue to resonate with nearly everyone:

1. Start college
2. Join a club during freshmen or sophomore year
3. Look for an internship junior year
4. Attend the fall career fair as a senior
5. Start applying for jobs with increasing frequency as graduation nears

Sound familiar? We're not saying this is wrong, but you're putting A LOT of pressure on yourself to close a deal and land your first post-college job in a short amount of time. And let's be clear here, this book is dedicated to helping you find the job you want, not the job you feel *stuck* with because time ran out and your rent's due next week.

If we think about the job application process for a second, it reminds us of an everyday situation. Say you meet someone at a coffee shop, a bar, or anywhere. Imagine that after a couple minutes of meaningless chitchat, that person asks you for a favor. How likely are you to help out this stranger? More often than not, you'll make a quick excuse and remove yourself from the situation. But what if a friend came to you and said, "Hey, I'm short $20 bucks. Can you help me?" You always say yes. You're willing to help someone out because they're your friend and you know them. Maybe they pay you back and help you when you need it, or maybe they don't, but either way you still chip in. The same can be applied here. If you genuinely connect with someone in an industry in which you may want to work (a.k.a. your first job), when the time comes for advice or a recommendation, or even a job, you'll have someone in your corner helping you out. Just like Jason helped out Dan.

When we asked Dan how he typically likes to meet new people, we initially suggested "networking events," to which he laughed out loud. His advice is to avoid these events at all costs, which we would also recommend. Instead, meet one-on-one for a coffee and begin to build that relationship. Talk about what excites you, what you're working towards, why you reached out to them, or all of the above. Your odds of forging a meaningful relationship will be much greater one-on-one than at a giant networking event. If you want to be surrounded by a bunch of people all asking the same generic questions, just go to a bar, spare yourself the uncomfortable dress clothes, and relax in normal clothes with a drink.

There is one last point, which needs to be stressed: Don't spam.

If you're spamming people with generic messages, and not acting sincere when requesting someone's time, you're going to have difficulty getting any responses. When it comes to building meaningful relationships, quality over quantity will work to your advantage, and it certainly has worked out well for Dan, Justin, ourselves, and so many more.

OUR CHALLENGE

CHAPTER TWENTY-THREE

SO NOW WHAT?

DO SOMETHING

Interview after interview, inspiration after inspiration. Everyone was different and everyone had a story. As we wrote this book, we found a common denominator among all of these people who did something a little crazy and took a few risks. They are now sitting at the head of the table in seats of success. Between a middle-aged woman putting Christmas lights on her house and the hustler who signed up customers before even working for the company, there's a common thread. They all did something. SOMETHING! And the funny thing is that even the people who did SOMETHING and didn't even get the job (Kendra with her Lego resume, Alice's letter to Instagram) still saw results and benefits.

We've done our best to share these techniques so you can replicate them for yourself, but what it all comes down to is using the skills you know and making sure there is relevance within the company you're pursuing. Victor, with the QR Code resume, said it nicely in his interview, "If you are attempting a creative technique to find a job, your technique better be true to the codes and DNA of the companies to whom you are applying."

When talking with Matthew Epstein about his googlehire.me viral video, he emphasized that people will not be successful copying the same technique he did. In fact, many people tried to replicate it and were not successful. His suggestion for people was to stay within their skillset and passion when performing a creative technique. He said, "Do what you love, and your passion will be seen."

Everyone can do SOMETHING. All of our interviewees knew what they wanted to do. They had a passion about a career path or a certain company. They were specific with what they wanted and where they focused their efforts. And by doing this they saw results—each and every one of them.

This book is about giving you a shot. We don't guarantee a job, but we will get your resume in front of a human, rather than just a robot. And we can assure you that you have no shot with a robot! Even if you are qualified and passionate, you're leaving it up to an algorithm. If you wanted to gamble, we'd tell you to hit the casino to try and win your life's fortune. But if you want to take control and get in front of the right people, you've just taken the biggest step towards making that happen by reading this book.

Quit being embarrassed! Quit feeling like an annoyance! Trust us, everyone we interviewed threw those feelings out the window a long time ago, and look at their results. They speak for themselves.

CHAPTER TWENTY-FOUR

OUR CHALLENGE

E veryone we interviewed decided they were ready to take the challenge. Nothing was a sure shot, but they put themselves out there and set their pride aside. For them, in one way or another what they did paid off. It was not easy. This book is not about the fastest or easiest way to land a job. This book is about hard work, passion, and determination. And at the end of the day, **this book is about results.**

Our "challenge" is defined as doing something in an attempt to get your resume in front of a human being. This could be a technique we have mentioned in the book or something you have come up with entirely on your own. Graeme (viral video) said it perfectly: "I thought that if I'm bored writing my own CV, how bored is my audience going to be?" So don't be boring. Instead, get *noticed*, and get *hired*.

If you decide to take this challenge, we are dying to hear and share your story. We want to know how bold you got! We want the good, the bad, and the ugly. Just as important as it is to know what worked, we want to know what didn't work.

Please go to the "CHALLENGE" section of our website (www. boldjobbook.com) and tell us about it. Not only will you inspire others and help them through their job search process, but it will also give you a chance to win prizes for the best (and worst!) monthly challenges.

This is just the beginning. We have barely scratched the surface with these twenty three stories from people all around the world. There is so much more to be learned, and we need your help to do so. Best of luck, and remember: Be **BOLD**, get noticed, get hired.

Made in the USA
Monee, IL
21 October 2020